A PERSONAL HISTORY OF THE KETTERING TOWN CRICKET LEAGUE

Dave Short

Published by Dan Publishing

Copyright © Dave Short

ISBN: 0-9550763-0-7

In memory of my son, Robert.

This book is also dedicated to my grandchildren: Emily, Matthew, Georgina, Jenna and my youngest grandson Jacob (the greatest footballer in the world), who is destined to become the greatest cricketer in the world.

Acknowledgements

I would like to thank John Hill, Carl Howard and Paul Rowney for encouraging me to write this book, and also for their help in producing it.

I have spent endless months at the Evening Telegraph sifting through back copies of their newspaper, and I am deeply indebted to Liz MacBride for her support and assistance. Grateful thanks to the staff at Kettering Public Library and the Kettering Museum for their help and guidance.

Thank you to all those who furnished me with scorebooks, photographs, Handbooks, old dinner menus and other memorabilia. These included: Dave Walker, Dave Chaplin, Gordon Hilliard, Dennis Hefford, Reg Green, Artie Isham, Pat Brookes, Brian Munton, Malc Briggs, Mick Beasley, Eddie Armstrong, Ron York, Colin Smith, Arnie Fox, Terry Wright, Reg Abbott, Billy Mann, Maurice Tyrrell, Fred Beasley, Fred Blount, Norman Cooper, Russell Prentice, John Lawman, Bob Miller, Barry Cartwright, Ray Patrick, Len Hope and Norman Goodfellow.

I am also indebted to Brian Osborn for kindly loaning me the minute book of the Kettering Cricket Association.

My thanks also to Dudley Wallis of Little Harrowden Cricket Club who allowed me to take away the Edgar Towell Challenge Trophy which, as the last winners of the six-a-side, had been in their possession since 1994.

Finally, to my two daughters Tracy and Jane, my sons-in-law Neil and Peter and my long suffering wife Ann (for having to put up with the incessant droning of the computer and endless ringing of the telephone). Without their help and support this book would have been impossible to produce.

CONTENTS

Foreword

It was almost three years ago that I heard from a long forgotten source that Dave Short was writing a history of the Kettering Town Cricket League. I remember thinking that it was absolutely marvellous that someone was prepared to offer the necessary time, effort and dedication to spend countless hours studying the Evening Telegraph archives, the records at both the Kettering Museum and the Kettering Public Library, in addition to contacting many dozens of players and official for information relating to the cricket history of Kettering between 1912 and 1993.

Writing a book can be a most tedious job, needing quite an incentive to keep going, and in producing this history, David's incentive was to be found in the enjoyment of seeing his work developing, finally being published and ready for sale – rather than being concerned whether sales would reach 5,000 copies! It was the hard work; the research, being involved, meeting old cronies, making new friends and finally seeing the work evolve that attracted him.

All Town Leaguers should be proud to be a part of his work, whether or not they are named within these pages. Without their joint efforts upon the playing fields of Kettering, this volume could not represent such a laudable contribution to the social history of Kettering Town.

Well done Dave, and thank you!

CARL HOWARD – JULY 2005
KETTERING TOWN CRICKET LEAGUE 1954 – 1983

Introduction

I have been pre-occupied with this book for the best part of three years. It has been an enjoyable experience, whilst at the same time a very challenging and frustrating and one.

The challenge came from visiting many places listed below and sifting through documents and newspapers in order to glean appropriate information on the Town League. My sources were the Kettering Library, Northamptonshire Evening Telegraph, Kettering Museum as well as old score books, photographs and handbooks that people kindly loaned to me. I also interviewed many people who were able to furnish me with some very useful information, for which I am deeply grateful.

However, the frustration came from not being able to validate some of the information given. A couple of players told me that they recorded centuries in the league. Unfortunately, they could not remember the year in which they did this or whom their opponents were, and I could not find the appropriate records. So, although I feel that this book is as accurate an account of the league that I could hope to get, I have to concede that there may be a few omissions.

The last ten years has seen a major overhaul take place in local cricket in Northamptonshire. The County League has become much more structured and can now boast many leagues with some hundred or so teams taking part, with a system of promotion and relegation in place. This restructuring has proved to be very beneficial to teams who own their own ground. It has allowed them to move up to an, arguably, higher level of cricket. To do this, most of them have had to improve their grounds and the facilities that they offer. So for these teams, it has proved a great success and it will hopefully lead to more homegrown players making it to the very top. Teams from the old Kettering and District League and the Mid Northants Village League are now to be seen playing in the County League - they were able to do this because they had brought their grounds up to County League standards. Town League sides did not have this option, as when the league decided to disband it was not just the league that was finished, it was also the end of the road for the teams too, as without their own ground they had nowhere to go.

Sadly, I fear that the Town League will never come back, it has served its purpose, it belonged to another time and has no place in the hurly burly of today's progressive way of life. Many people mourned its passing and many still do to this day. It had its place in time and it reflected a way of life that I fear will also not return. However, for those of us who were fortunate enough to play in the Town League, we are left with nothing but happy memories.

Chapter I

1912-1919

*And hold the bat again, as when a boy,
and face a Myriad bowlers without fear,
Were I not old.*

D. I. A. Jephson.

1912

The Town League began in 1912. The founder members were: Kettering
Men's Own Institute, Kettering Working Men's II, Miss Butchers Bible
Class, Kettering Midland Railway, Kettering Co-op Clothiers, St Mary's
Bible Class, Kettering Electricians, The Church Institute and Fuller Bible
Class. The first president of the league was Mr. Charles Saunders who was a
partner in the well-known firm of architects Gotch and Saunders, the
chairman was Mr. W.H.Brockhurst who was an accountant, and the league's
first secretary was Mr. A. Kilsby

The first season produced some interesting cricket with some fine
individual performances. In the match between St Mary's BC and the Co-op
Clothiers, St Mary's scored 101-9 and in reply the Co-op scored 119-8, with
T. Freeman scoring 68 for the Co-op and H. Freestone taking 6 wickets for
St Mary's.

As the season progressed two teams dominated the proceedings,
Men's own Institute and the Working Men's – they were neck and neck in
the race to become the first winners of the league. The weather had been
particularly unkind so much so that a special management meeting was
called to discuss the situation, two representatives from each team in the
league were present. The issue at hand was loss of matches due to poor
weather. A proposition was put forward whereby the Men's Own and the
Working Men's should play a deciding match with the winners becoming
league champions. This proposal was defeated however and it was decided
that every attempt should be made to play all the matches lost to the weather
in September. This decision turned out to be a good one as the weather
improved considerably and some very exciting matches ensued.

The Men's Own had quite a shock against the Electricians when
they were bowled out for 44, but in reply the Electricians were bowled out
for 43. The Men's Own then went on to a comfortable victory over St
Mary's by 165 runs to 32, which was highlighted by a fine all round
performance from R. Masters, the Men's Own allrounder, who scored 62
runs and then went on to take 7 wickets. Meanwhile, the Working Men's

had a convincing win over Fuller by 107 runs to 31 runs with G. Coe taking 7 wickets for the Working Men's.

The final match of the season arrived with the Men's Own two points clear at the top of the table. Their opponents were Working Men's who were in second place, and the game certainly produced a fitting climax. The game was played on the 14th September and in fine sunny weather the Working Men's were bowled out for the lowly score of 44, the title seemed destined to go to the Men's Own. But the Working Men's stuck gamely to their task and, in a remarkable finish, bowled their opponents out for 43 to finish level with them at the top of the table. Thus the season finished with the Men's Own and the Working Men's being declared as joint champions. Some highly significant figures show that H. Towell and H. Smith took 93 wickets between them at an average of less than 4.00 for Men's Own and R. Sharp and G. Coe took 119 wickets at an average 5.00. for the Working Men's.

A dinner was held at the Cross Keys Hotel to celebrate the leagues first season. The Reverend T.G. Clarke presiding congratulated the league on a successful beginning and he then presented the medals to the two winning teams, with individual prizes going to F. Jeffrey (Men's Own) best batsman and to H. Towell (Men's Own) best bowler.

1913

St Mary's Bible class withdrew from the league and their place was taken by Mobbs and Lewis. Early scores indicated that, because of the appalling weather, teams were finding it extremely difficult to put any decent scores together. Midland Railway, replying to Miss Butchers score of 37, were bowled out for 20. Fuller fared no better being bowled out for 33, chasing the Men's Own score of 44. British Rail and Kettering Electricians began to put some good results together. Electricians scored 126 against Mobbs and Lewis and then bowled their opponents out for 125. Not to be outdone, the Railway exacted their revenge on Miss Butchers winning the return by 15 runs. T. Freeman was in fine form for Co-op Clothiers against Mobbs and Lewis, he scored 20 runs out of the Co-ops total of 60, and then he proceeded to take six Mobbs and Lewis wickets as they were bowled out for 29. Fuller beat last seasons joint champions, Working Men's club, by 31 runs – scores: Fuller 104, Working Men's Club 73. The Electricians and the Railway quickly left the other teams behind in the chase for the title, which eventually went to the Railmen by clear six points.

1914

Ten teams contested the league in 1914, Church Institute being the latest team to join. Two matches ended in ties - the game between Miss Butchers BC and Men's Own where both teams scored 49 runs with H. Towell taking 6 wickets for Men's Own, and the game between Midland Railway and Kettering Electricians which closed at 43 runs each.

F.Bull turned in a fine all-round performance for Mobbs and Lewis, scoring 75 runs out of their total of 143 and then taking 4 wickets as Fuller were dismissed for 80 runs. A low scoring game saw Miss Butchers BC triumph over Oakley BC by 34 runs to 29, with W. Askew taking 5 wickets for the Bible Class and W. Quincey taking 6 wickets for Miss Butchers. Men's Own lost a closely fought game to the Railway by eight runs – scores: Men's Own 56 Railway 64. Co-op Clothiers were bowled out for a miserly 16 runs against Oakley BC who had only set a target of 46, G. Loasby claiming 5 wickets for Oakley and G. Preston taking 6 wickets for the Co-op. Co-op Clothiers recorded a very good victory over the Railway, setting them a target of 44. They bowled the Railway out for 30, H. Freestone doing the damage by taking six wickets. Co-op Clothiers enjoyed a very successful season but they just failed to lift the title, which was eventually won by Miss Butchers.

1915

The season commenced with a challenge match between representatives of the Town League playing against Wellingborough Trades League, resulting in victory for the Wellingborough League by 151 runs to 46.

Back to the league action, and H. Marlow took 7 wickets for 7 runs for Miss Butchers BC against Working Men's II in another tied game 38 runs apiece. H. Chapman was having a great season with the ball for Working Men's, taking 7-22 against Oakley BC and 5-17 against Miss Butchers BC. Working Men's Club II needed to beat Mobbs and Lewis to clinch the title; they made a very good start, setting their opponents a target of 137. This was far too big a score for the last makers and they were bowled out for 53, to give the Works victory by 83 runs and their second league title.

A benefit match was played between the Athletic Club and a Town League eleven in aid of Horace Risely, who had broken his wrist whilst playing in a match (at this time the league did not insure its players, and you were only allowed to claim sick pay for injuries sustained at work).

1916-1919

Because of the outbreak of the First World War no Town League cricket took place during the period 1916-1919.

Chapter II

1920-1929

How shall we live, now that the summers ended,
And bat and ball (too soon!) are put aside.

Thomas Moult.

1920

It had taken the league the four years before the war to get themselves
properly established and they now found themselves having to start all over
again. Seven teams joined the league and it was decided to award two points
for a win, one for a tie and no points for a drawn game.

Miss Butchers and Fuller played out a low scoring game, with
Fuller just running out winners 43 runs to 40. Men's Own scored 92 against
Fuller and then bowled them out for 11. Oakley Bible Class and Kettering
Church Institute staged a thrilling game with Oakley BC running out winners
by one run, 50 runs to 49. But the team that really stood out was the Men's
Own Institute whom, following successive victories over Oakley BC, Fuller
and Working Men's II, won the title handsomely, and to confirm their
dominance they finished the season unbeaten.

1921

Remarkably, fourteen teams entered the league in 1921, which was an
increase of 100%. This was easily the most that had ever entered before.
Consequently, it was decided to form two divisions: A and B.

In Division A, the Athletic opened their campaign with an emphatic
victory over Oakley BC by 95 runs and they quickly established themselves
as favourites to win the league. They justified this position when they beat
Miss Butchers by 202 runs to 47, with F. Ellis scoring 56 and J. Piddington
scoring 43 to clinch the championship.

In Division B, Barton Wanderers dominated the league and it was
their batting which was their main strength; recording scores of over three
figures in most of their matches and winning the division with matches to
spare. A Championship match was played at the end of the season between
the Athletic and the Wanderers, and in an extremely good game victory went
to the Athletic by 149 runs to 129.

1922

After a record number of entries for the league last year no fewer than six
teams dropped out, significantly five of those were church affiliated teams.

The reason for this is not clear. So the season opened with eight teams taking part and there were some good individual performances.

After scoring 99 runs the Working Men's II skittled the Athletic II out for 26 with H. Draper and E. Bailey taking 5 wickets apiece. Athletic also fared badly against A Pickford who scored 67 runs for the Men's Own in their total of 137, to secure a winning margin of 88 runs. H. K. Wilson took 7-26 for the Wanderers against Athletic II, bowling them out for 54 to clinch an 83 run victory. However, bowling feat of the season was by H.K. Wilson who took 7 wickets for 3 (including a hat-trick) for the British Legion, who bowled out the Working Men's II for 23.

The quest for the title became a two horse race between the Wanderers and the Men's Own. The two teams met each other towards the end of the season. Men's Own took the honours winning the game by eight wickets. This was mainly due to H. Freeman who took 7 wickets in the Barton Wanderers score of 62 and A. Johnson who scored 30 not out in the Men's Own score of 64-2.

1923
There was no Town League cricket in 1923. The reason for this remains unclear.

1924
The season saw a titanic battle for the honours between the Men's Own and the North Park. The two teams were neck and neck throughout the season and the race culminated in both teams finishing the season on twenty-four points, both having won twelve of their fourteen matches. Amongst the Men's Own results were victories over the Working Men's II by 91 runs, and a nine wicket success over Trades II, in which H. Liquorish took 8 wickets for 14 runs. They then beat Miss Butchers by the overwhelming margin of 202 runs, F. Jeffrey and H. Liquorish scoring half centuries and T. Freeman taking 8 wickets for the victors.

Meanwhile North Park were defeating Miss Butchers by 38 runs, with A. Bailey taking 7-20 for the Park and following up with another 5 wickets in the return game. Their next game against the Electricians resulted in an emphatic win by 91 runs, and in a very close game North Park defeated their arch rivals Men's Own by 5 runs. Finally, the two teams played a deciding match for the championship, which was won by Men's Own.

1925
Only six teams entered the league this season, which was the lowest number since the league started. Another record was to be set; the North Park completing the season with a 100% record (played ten, won ten), a feat

never before achieved and one that would never be achieved in the Town League again. Miss Butchers finished as runners up, six points adrift of the champions. When the two teams met the result was a comfortable win for the North Park by 163 runs to 68, with P. Jeffcote scoring 58 for the Park. A. Biddlecombe had scores of 43 and 33 as the North Park continued to score heavily against all the teams in the league

1926

Mr. T. Banks was elected as secretary, and at the AGM he welcomed the nine teams that would be competing for the honours. Amongst the nine, there were two new clubs; S.Patrick and J. Hutchens. S. Patrick sent out warning signals to the rest of the league with an easy victory over Hutchens by 130 runs, with H. Riseley scoring 50. They followed this up with a 58 run win against Miss Butchers, with G. Martin and E. Walpole taking five wickets a piece. Patricks managed to maintain their form throughout the season and they clinched the title when they beat St Andrews 129-40.

Mr. Steve Patrick, Chairman of Patrick, was so pleased with the team's success that he arranged a celebration dinner. Guest of honour was Mr. Charles Saunders, the League President, who congratulated the team on winning the league at their first attempt and presented shields to all the players. The Evening Telegraph reported that the evening was highly successful and that Miss Atwell, W. Eagle jr., Mr. C. Martin, Mr. Clipston, Mr. R. Brown and the Chairman himself, Mr. S. Patrick, sang songs. At the conclusion of the singing there were three rousing cheers for the host Mr. S. Patrick.

1927

Once again there were nine teams battling for the honours. There was an early blow for last years champions, S. Patricks, who suffered their first defeat in the league when they were beaten by the Co-op Clothiers by 28 runs. Another good result followed for the Clothiers when they soundly beat the Athletic II by 126 runs to 45, thanks to a fine all-round performance by I. Tomalin who scored 45 runs and then went on to take 5 wickets. Despite their early setback, Patricks quickly got back into their stride and reeled off a string of victories, which enabled them to retain the title, the first team to do so. Co-op Clothiers finished as runners up, nine points adrift of the winners.

There was a Champions v The Rest match to conclude the season, with Patricks underlining their strength by defeating the rest by 123 runs to 105.

1928

Patricks were chasing a third successive championship and they set about their task with great determination. They quickly gave notice of their intentions with a string of early victories. They rattled up a massive score of 234 against Hutchens, E Groome scoring 72, and then dismissed their opponents for 84. They followed this with an impressive 92 run victory against Wrights, with A.Walpole and G. Martin scoring 62 and 46 respectively, with R. Groome taking 6-9 when Wrights batted.

Thomas Birds also started well with victories over North Park and St Andrews. Against the latter, they scored 180 runs with F. Dickenson and M.Sherbourne both scoring 69.

Another team to prosper was St Mary's, and it was they who kept pace with Patricks, with both teams finishing the season on the same number of points. In the ensuing play off for the title, victory went to St Mary's who, in a low scoring game, won by 60 runs to 33.

1929

At the Annual General Meeting, it was decided to have two divisions: A and B. The winners of each division would play a deciding match, the winner of which would be declared the champions.

There was an amazing match between Fuller and Miss Butchers. Fuller were bowled out for 54 with B. Skinner taking 5-21, and in reply Miss Butchers were bowled out for 16 with J. Newman taking 8 wickets. But the most astonishing thing was that Miss Butchers opening batsman A. Panter carried his bat for 10 not out. Co-op Clothiers had a surprising victory by 52 runs over Birds who could only muster 26 runs in their innings, due to the bowling of H. Capps 5-11 and J. Mason 5-8. Freeman Hardy and Willis were dominating the A Division due, in no small part, to the batting of Maurice Dunkley who made some good scores; including 58 against Working Men's. It came as no surprise when they finished top of the Division. A Course turned in a fine all round performance for Gravestocks scoring 69 not out in a total of 117, and then taking 4 wickets as Leader Sports were bowled out for 101.

Miss Butchers recovered from their disastrous game against Co-op to put a string of good results together and finish the season as winners of Division B. The Championship decider was a disappointing affair with Freeman Hardy and Willis running out winners by 124 runs to 44, due to the excellent bowling of W. Woolmer who returned figures of 8-16 for the shoe-men.

This year was a very important year for cricket in Kettering as it saw the introduction of the Kettering Knock Out Cup. The competition was organised by the Kettering Cricket Association, an organisation that was

18

formed to foster the game of cricket locally and to improve the facilities for players and encourage young people to take up the game.

Men's Own and Working Men's Club contested the first final and a crowd of three hundred people turned out to watch the proceedings. Victory went to the Men's Own who scored 110-5 with L. Tomalin scoring 47 and H. Licquorish 25. In reply, the Works gave a good account of themselves, scoring 101-9, with W. Garley scoring 25 and L. Hales taking 5-17 for the Men's Own. Mr. Charles Saunders, the President of the Association, presented the cup to the winning captain and congratulated both sides on a memorable first final. He also said that he thought the competition would greatly enhance local cricket.

Chapter III

1930-1939

Grass at our feet, and the sun overhead,
Here let us play till the evening is red.

E.V. Lucas

1930

Twelve Teams contested the league and again they were split up into two
sections, A and B, with six teams in each league. Officers elected were;
President: Mr. Charles Saunders, Secretary: Mr. C.Rainbow, Treasurer: Mr.
F. Smith and Chairman: Mr. R. Sharp. The champions of Division I were
Freeman Hardy and Willis, and St Mary's Bible Class took the second
Division title. Highlight of the season was the bowling of O. Pearson who
became the first player in the history of the Town League to take all ten
wickets in a match, when he took ten wickets for twelve runs for North Park
in their match against Thomas Birds.

The Knock Out cup was won by the Men's Own, who beat
Crusaders in the final, by 88 runs to 60. The game was watched by an
estimated eight hundred people. This was the period when the Town League
really came of age, good individual and team performances were being
achieved and the standard of cricket being produced was finally being
recognised. This was highlighted by the attendance figures for the Knock
Out competition.

1931

St Andrews BC and St Mary's BC resigned from the league to join the
District League. While, sadly, one of the leagues most successful teams, S.
Patricks, could not raise a team. An application from Havelock Works to join
the league was accepted. Freeman Hardy and Willis defeated Miss Butchers
BC 111 runs to 55 with Maurice Dunkley, the famous Manchester City and
Northampton footballer (and later to represent the county at cricket), scoring
65 runs for the shoemen. Working Men's Club rattled up an impressive 205
against Leader Sports and then A. Smith took 6-14 to bowl the Sports out for
39.

Other notable achievements included; Mobbs and Lewis bowling
out North Park II for 49 with T. Coleman taking six wickets, and WMC
bowling F. Millers out for 21, with A. Hodgett taking six wickets. After a
closely fought contest, WMC were crowned as champions with Thomas
Birds finishing as runners up.

21

Men's Own and North Park met in the first semi-final of the Knock Out Cup. North Park batted first and put together a more than useful score of 137-7, with B. Drew scoring 54 and N. Perrot 45. In reply, Men's Own scored 85, E. Bailey taking 6-41. The other semi-final was a much closer affair between William Timpsons and St Mary's. Timpsons batted first and scored 108 with Chater scoring 24 not out, St Mary's made a determined attempt to get the runs but they fell 17 runs short. The final was an exciting affair. North Park batted first and were bowled out for 69, N. Perrot scored 25, with Thorpe claiming 6 wickets for Timpsons. In reply a valiant effort by B. Smith (he carried his bat throughout the innings for 38) was to no avail as Timpsons were bowled out for 61. E. Bailey took 5 wickets for North Park who ran out worthy winners.

1932

Only six teams entered the league this year and the eventual winners were Thomas Birds. They narrowly won the title from Freeman Hardy's, who in their last game of the season were bowled out for 44 against WMC, with A. Sherbourne taking six wickets.

The Knock Out Cup Final was played between Kettering Evening XI and Frank Wrights. Each side batted for seventy minutes, with Frank Wrights running out winners by 139 runs to 92. The highlight of the Frank Wrights innings was the 96 not out scored by W. King (which still remains the highest score ever made in a Knock out Final). The attendance was estimated at several thousand, which prompted Mr. A. Joyce who presented the trophies, to say how pleased the County Club would be to receive such a wonderful gate.

1933

It was a good summer, weather wise, and the batsmen took full advantage of the sunny conditions with some quite excellent individual performances. Maurice Dunkley scored 102 out of a total of 250 for Freeman Hardy and Willis against Miss Butchers, resulting in a 169 run victory. Bert Russell went one run better than Maurice scoring 103 for Havelock Works against T. Birds, who thanks to F. Garley (61 runs) and A Cartwright (50 runs), ran out winners by 29 runs. Wilson and Watsons won the league by four points from Freeman Hardy and Willis.

The Knock out Cup Final was played between Freeman Hardy and Willis and Frank Wrights. It was watched by a crowd of three thousand people, and what an extraordinary game it was! Batting first, Freeman Hardy and Willis scored 128 -5 in their allotted time with Maurice Dunkley scoring 70 not out. In reply, Frank Wrights scored 136-4 to win a memorable game and so retain the trophy they won last year.

1934

Eight teams would be competing in the league this year among them were two newcomers; London Congregational and Smith and Fosters. Bert Russell made a good start to the season for Havelock Works taking 7-12 against T. Birds, who were bowled out for 64 to give Havelock victory by 42 runs. Smith and Fosters made a good start to their league campaign by bowling out Freeman Hardy and Willis for 29, with Blanchard taking 6-14 and C.Norman 4-15, to secure a narrow victory by 3 runs. The championship finally went to Havelock Works who consolidated after a good start to the season.

This year a Champions versus the Rest of the League game was staged and resulted in an overwhelming win for the Rest. The scores were the Rest 161, Havelock Works 26, highlighted by a fine all round performance for The Rest by Bill Dunham of Mobbs and Lewis, who scored 49 runs and then took 4 Havelock wickets for 14. Len Shipley took the other 6 for 14 runs.

The Knock out Cup Final once again featured Frank Wrights who made it a hat trick of wins by defeating Timpson by 19 runs. Chief architect of their victory was B. Wright who took 6-15.

1935

Wilson and Watsons piled on the runs against Miss Butchers scoring an impressive 172, with S. Gilbert scoring 50. Despite A. Hunt and B. Skinner scoring 43 and 48 respectively for the Bible Class, they were all out for 122. Another useful score by Wilson and Watsons of 162 this time (with J. Riddle scoring 49 and A. Hunt making 50), saw them beat Kaycee comfortably by 79 runs. J. Riddle rounded off a good match by taking 7-22. They found themselves up against it though, when chasing Mobbs and Lewis mediocre score of 95. They were bowled out single handed for 92 by the spin of Bill Dunham, who took all 10 wickets for 48 runs.

Miss Butchers and Gravestocks had an exciting match with Miss Butchers running out the winners by one run. The scores were: Miss Butchers 63 Gravestocks 62. A. Panter and B. Skinner taking 4 wickets apiece for Miss Butchers. It was Thomas Birds, however, who dominated proceedings in their match with Wilson and Watsons. They made 111-5 with A. Cartwright making 46 and Fred Garley 25. Then, M. Sherbourne took 4-16 as Wilson and Watsons were dismissed for 85 runs. A much closer game followed when they took on Freeman Hardy and Willis. Batting first, Birds scored 116 runs and they then bowled out FHW for 104 despite Maurice Dunkley scoring 56 (Len Shipley took 5-29). Altogether, Birds were too strong for the rest and they went on to win the league with Wilson and Watsons taking the runners up spot. At the end of the season, a match was played between the Champions, Thomas Birds and the Rest of the League, with the Rest coming out victors by 77 runs to 51, George Meadows taking 5-13 for the Champions and A. Hunt 6-10 for the Rest.

Len Shipley was also in good form in the Knock out Cup, he took 8 wickets for 6 runs (which included a hat trick) as Birds beat Clarence by 60 runs. In the second round he went one better claiming 9-23 as Wilson and Watsons were knocked out of the competition. It was William Timpsons, however, appearing in their third final, who won the Cup beating Kettering. The scores were William Timpsons 97-9 (W. Smith 23. R. Wooster 7-44) Kettering 76-9 (J. Andrews 4 wickets, W. Thorpe 3 wickets). Councillor C. Mayes presented the cup and the crowd was estimated as lining the ground several people deep.

1936

The season opened with a challenge match between the Kettering Town League and the Wellingborough Town League and victory went to the Kettering team by 80 runs to 54, Bill Dunham took 5-20, Albert Smith 3-13 and Len Shipley 2-13.

Miss Butchers BC owed a lot to the fine bowling of B. Skinner and Albert Smith who between them took 93 wickets at an average of 7.00. B. Skinner took 6 wickets in bowling out Kaycee for 24, and another 6 against Wilson and Watsons dismissing them for 44. Len Shipley took 7-45 against Wilson and Watsons who scored 102 all out. In reply, Birds could only muster 85. Miss Butchers were in great form, they ran up a score of 151 against Mobbs and Lewis and then bowled their opponents out for 79. When they met Gravestocks they beat them by 131 runs to 79 with Albert Smith scoring 56 not out. It was then the turn of Wilson and Watsons who were dismissed for 44. B. Skinner taking 6 wickets to see Miss Butchers home, but not without a fright as they struggled against some tight bowling, eventually winning by 4 wickets.

Albert Smith proved himself to be an all rounder to be reckoned with by finishing with a batting average of 17.00. It was not surprising then that Miss Butchers won the league.

The Town won the Knock Out Cup when they defeated Crusaders in the final. Town batted first and scored 123-6, with H.J.H. Lamb scoring 53 and K.R. Greasley scoring 40. In reply, Crusaders could only manage a score of 26, with Edgar Towell claiming seven Crusaders wickets for ten runs including a hat trick. In one of the earlier rounds, R. Steventon of the Athletic returned the remarkable figures of 9 wickets for 2 runs against the Teachers, who could only manage a miserable 26 runs.

1937

The season kicked off with a challenge match between the League and their counter parts from Wellingborough, resulting in victory for Wellingborough by 108 runs to 59. However, Albert Smith turned in another fine all round performance scoring 38 runs and taking 4 wickets for 26. In the league, Bert Russell had a good match against Stocks, scoring 38 runs and then taking 6-8 to dismiss them for 22.

Another fine bowling display was recorded by Bill Dunham of Mobbs and Lewis, who took 6-12 when they dismissed Freeman Hardy and Willis for 39, and went on to win the match by 23 runs. Miss Butchers looked to be in trouble when Kaycee bowled them out for 41 runs, with H. Sculthorpe taking 5 wickets. But thanks to B. Skinner, who took 6 wickets, Kaycee succumbed for just 17 runs. Jim Law took 8-18 as Mobbs and Lewis triumphed over Kaycee by 32 runs. L. Cullip made a very good 63 for Miss Butchers as they saw off Wilson & Watson by 28 runs. It seemed that no one could stop Miss Butchers and they went on to win the league for the second successive year.

Freeman Hardy and Willis and Kettering Thursday contested the final of the Knock Out Cup at the North Park. Freeman Hardys batted first and set a target of 96 with Reg Green scoring 47 runs. In reply, their opponents made a gallant attempt but fell short by just 9 runs, Harold Chapman taking four wickets for the Mill Road team.

1938

Sixteen teams applied to join the league in 1938 and, rather surprisingly, there were nine teams in Div I and seven in Div II. A fine spell of bowling from Len Shipley and George Meadows of T. Birds saw last years champions, Miss Butchers, dismissed for 69 runs, with the two fast bowlers claiming five wickets each. However, in reply, Birds could only manage a total of 60 runs due, no doubt, to the bowling of L. Cullip who took 8-17. G. Wallington scored 114 for Gravestocks in their total of 190 against Wilson and Watsons who were then bowled out for 62 (W. Reed taking 6-13). In their next match, Gravestocks amassed an amazing 271 with W. Julian the centurion this time scoring 101. Their opponents, Gas Co, were then bowled out for 67 with that man Julian capping a great day by claiming 4-22. The first Division title race was once again won by Miss Butchers BC to complete a hat trick of titles, a feat never before achieved.

Gravestocks and Barton Wanderers finished the season level on points and a play off was needed to decide the second division championship. The winners were Barton Wanderers who won a low scoring game by 65 runs to 43 (L. Weatherall took 7-20). Notable achievements during the season were: F.Julian of Gravestocks who won both the batting and the bowling averages in Div II.

The awards were as follows;

Division I Batting: A. Goodhall. (Miss Butchers) Average 32.68
Division I Bowling: A. Smith (Miss Butchers) Average at 5.57
Division II Batting: F. Julian (Gravestocks) Average 39.72
Division II Bowling: F. Julian. (Gravestocks) Average 39.72

Bill Dunham of Mobbs and Lewis was runner up in both the batting and the bowling in the First Division.

The Knock Out Final was between Havelock Works and Mobbs and Lewis. In a very exciting final Havelock Works batted first and scored 83-9 with Bert Russell scoring 29 and C. Wright 25. In reply, Mobbs and Lewis managed to scrape home by one wicket.

1939

At the Annual General Meeting, it was decided to introduce eight ball overs in the coming season. There were two tied matches during the season: Wilson and Watsons and Kaycee scoring 64 runs each and T. Birds II and the Gas Company finishing level on 93 runs apiece. For Mobbs and Lewis, Bill Dunham put in a fine spell of bowling against Freeman Hardy and Willis taking 8-28 in their total of 71, but in reply the last makers could only muster 22 runs with A. Frost taking 6-6. Captained by A. Cartwright, Thomas Birds made a determined bid to stop Miss Butchers from winning the league for the fourth successive time. It was touch and go right up to the last game with Birds just taking the title. Gravestock won the second Division, with Mobbs and Lewis taking the runners up spot. The league batting and bowling averages were won respectively by:

Division I Batting: C. Freestone (Miss Butchers)
Division I Bowling: A. Frost (Freeman Hardy and Willis).
Division II Batting: H. Bell (Thomas Birds)
Division II Bowling: J. Butler (Thomas Birds)

In the return match Reg Green scored 105 runs for Freeman Hardy and Willis in their match against Mobbs and Lewis.

Freeman Hardy and Willis were the winners of the Kettering Association Knock Out Cup.

During the season the world was once again thrown into turmoil with the outbreak of the Second World War. Sadly the league would lose three of its officers during the war period, President Mr. C. Saunders,

Secretary Mr. C Rainbow and Chairman Mr. R. Sharpe. Many teams would never play in the league again, most notably Miss Butchers Bible Class who had been the most successful team to date.

Nomads: Winners of the Kettering Association Knock Out Cup1946
Back row (l to r): A. Loasby, S. Tyrell, F. Loasby, G. Sheffield, Not Known, B Mann
Front Row: B. Lee, A Chapman, P. Wall, P. Skinner, J. Lee, S.Waller

Action from the Six-A-Side Tournament at the North Park circa 1957

Fuller: Town League Champions 1950
Back Row (l to r): D. Hope, R. Flecknor, A. Small, J.Chaplin, B.Payne, N.Wardle, R. Holding, F. Smith, D. Barlow
Front Row: D Hefford, Mr. Newman, J. Bent, B. Munton, M.Walker

Dolcis: Town League Champions 1947
Back Row (l to r): Not Known, J. Hawthorne, R. Boddington, D. Walker, C. Ingram, B. Garrett, Not Known, L. Shipley, Not Known
Front Row: H. Sharp, A. Lawrence, A. Cartwright, G. Swales, H. Bell

British Railways: Division II B Champions and Winners of the Association
Knock Out Cup 1952
Back Row (l to r): L. Fisher, D. Buckby, L. Burton, T. Clarke, L. Plews
Front Row: G. Beasley, A. Isham, H. Marlow, F. Loasby, R Walpole

Presentation Evening at the Cross Keys Café 1950
(l to r): A. Cartwright (Div. I Batting - Dolcis), L.Small (Div.II Batting - Timpsons),
Mr. T. Bird (President), P. Corbett (Div. II Bowling - Nomads),
D. Chaplin (Div.I Bowling - Mens Own)

Kaycee 1958: Town League Division II Champions 1958
Back Row (l to r): C. Howard, J. Hollis, R. Darlow,
R. Tarry, D. Dunkley, R. Toseland
Front Row: E. Armstrong, B Brown, R. Sanders, A. Johnson

Casuals Cricket Club Team Photograph circa 1948
Back Row (l to r): S. Richards, W. Chester, A. Shepherd, R. Patrick, G. Broughton,
F. Lawrence, L. Richards (Scorer)
Front Row: R. Keller, R. Drew, J. Bradshaw, R. York, C. Richards, E. Palmer

Dolcis: Going Out To Field circa 1950

Holyoake: One of the leagues longest serving members taken in 1978
Back Row: L/R: J. Hillyard, B. Ashby, F. Drewry, A. Ashby,
M. Beasley, J. Shelton, I. Mason
Front Row: E. Ashby (scorer), D. Strangeward, J. Hill, R. Bacon,
R. Dolby, G. Shelton

Tudors: Town League Champions 1978
Back Row (l to r): G. Beasley (Umpire), P. Cross, M. Chapman, D. Lewis,
D. Short, R. Ashby, P Rowney
Front Row: M. Briggs, R. Smith, B. Isham, C. Glanfield, J. Kelly

Havelock Works: Town League Champions 1934

Chapter IV

1940-1949

I'll goo and we'll set up a wicket
An we'll have a good innens at cricket.

William Barnes

1940

Despite the war the league continued until clubs found themselves unable to raise teams. There would again be two leagues - A and B. St Mary's enjoyed a very successful season winning Division A, with William Timpsons finishing in second place. A very exciting game took place when St Mary's and Timpsons met towards the end of the season. St Mary's batted first and scored 118, with Harold Townsend scoring 35 and C. Goode 32. In reply, Timpsons were three runs short of their opponents on 115, with J. Taylor scoring 42. In Division B, Kaycee, Freeman Hardy and Willis and J. P. Booths were all in contention to win the league. It went right down to the final game with the honours eventually going to Freeman Hardy and Willis.

William Timpsons and Kettering Thursday United opposed each other in the Knockout Cup final in what proved to be an excellent game. Timpsons batted first and put together a score of 105-7, with P. Rowley scoring 63. Kettering Thursday made a valiant attempt to get the runs thanks to E. Lewin who made 44 runs, but they failed by just 7 runs to reach their target. There was an estimated crowd of 2,000 watching the match and a collection realised seven pounds for hospital funds.

1941

Because of the war, it was too difficult for most clubs to raise a team every week so the decision was made to suspend the League for the time being. It was decided, however, to play the Knock Out Cup and there were a good number of entries received. Eventually, they got down to the last four and St Mary's beat William Timpsons in the first semi-final, and Men's Own beat Gravestocks in the other semi-final. The final was played at the North Park playing field in front of a fair sized crowd. The Men's Own batted first and made a creditable total of 93-7, with Stan Hodges making 20 and R. Chapman also making 20. In reply, St Mary's made a very spirited 87 all out, with Rogers hitting a quick fire 27 with two sixes and a four. However, it was all in vain, as George Walklate took 5-43 and B. Brew took 5-37 to round off a very good final.

29

1942

Men's Own and William Timpsons contested the first semi-final in the Knock Out Cup and victory went to Men's Own. In the other semi-final Rothwell Town proved to be too strong for the RA (Army). Rothwell batted first and scored 94-6, with Johnson scoring 40 not out. The army team could only manage a total of 59, with E. Crook taking 6-22. The final between Men's Own and Rothwell was a bizarre affair taking three matches to complete. In the first game, after eighteen overs the scores were level on 87 runs to each side. It was decided that the match should be replayed on the following Saturday. Men's Own batted first and scored 119, in reply Rothwell had progressed to 70-8 when torrential rain forced the game to be abandoned. A third game took place and this time, it was completed; Men's Own ran out the winners by 7 runs.

1943

The Royal Electrical and Mechanical Engineers and the 4th Northants Home Guard contested the first semi-final of the Knock Out cup and it turned out to be a rather one sided affair. The Home Guard batted first and managed to put together a score of 87, with L. C. Smith scoring 20. They then bowled out the REME for 51, with Weatherall claiming 6-28 and L/C Smith 4-11.

In the other semi-final, Men's Own played the Northants Fire Service. Batting first the Men's Own scored 79, with Trev Coleman making 20. In reply, the firemen scored only 48 due in no small part to Edgar Towell, who took 7-21. The final proved to be a personal triumph for Edgar Towell and P. A. Wright who took five wickets apiece as the Men's Own dismissed Home Guard for 61, and it was just a formality as Men's Own knocked off the runs for the loss of five wickets.

1944

A Royal Airforce XI met the REME in the first semi-final. After winning the toss they elected to bat first and scored a useful 84 runs, Sgt. Goodey making the best contribution with 27 runs. When the REME batted they had no answer to the bowling of Cpl. Dickenson who took 6-8 and they were dismissed for a disappointing 25 runs.

Men's Own and the Home Guard clashed in the other semi-final. Men's Own batted first and thanks to A. Gosden 59 and C. Freestone 43, they scored an impressive 123-3. Lt. Lewis scored a spirited 43 for the Home Guard but it was not enough and they were eventually all out for 83. In the final, the RAF XI batted first and scored 117-7. In reply, the Men's Own could only muster 66-7, a very disappointing final.

1945

William Timpsons again reached the semi-final stage of the Knock Out Cup and this time their opponents were the RAF (Maintenance). RAF batted first and scored 96. Timpsons reply was disappointing as they could only come up with a score of 61. Last years winners, Men's Own, were beaten in the other semi-final by Geddington. Geddington batted first in the final and scored a very modest 74, thanks to a valuable contribution of 26 from Henson. When the RAF batted Longhurst, the Geddington opening bowler, performed superbly to send five RAF batsmen back to the pavilion for 22 runs. The RAF never recovered from this early onslaught and were eventually dismissed for 71 runs to give Geddington victory by a margin of 3 runs.

1946

The first Annual General Meeting of the league since 1939 was held on the twenty fifth of March. Two minutes silence was held in remembrance of all the players and officials that had died during the war. New officials were duly elected and they were as follows:

President: Mr. Thomas Bird
Chairman: Mr. Reg Banks
Secretary: Mr C. Swales
Treasurer: Mr. T. Smith.

It was decided not to continue with the eight ball over, introduced in 1939, but to revert back to the six ball over. Annual subscriptions would be seven shillings and six pence (thirty-seven and a half pence). It was also decided to award three points for a win, one and a half for a tie and one point for a draw.

Six teams entered the league and Dolcis began very well, beating William Timpsons by 88 runs. The scores were: Dolcis 177-8 (A.Cartwright 78), Timpsons 89 (George Meadows 3-29 C. Ingram 3-1). Dolcis fared even better against Mobbs and Lewis scoring 200-3, with Dave Walker scoring 64 and Arthur Lawrence 74. When Mobbs and Lewis batted, Arthur Lawrence 4-4 and Chris Ingram 4-27 did the damage. Meanwhile, Freeman Hardy and Willis were beating Perfecta by 60 runs, thanks to Reg Green who scored 49 out of their total of 152. Dolcis dismissed Fuller for 48, thanks to George Meadows 5-29 and Len Shipley 3-8, to win the match comfortably by 5 wickets. After a bright start, Dolcis fell away rather dramatically and the eventual winners of the league were the Rifles

In the final of the Knock Out Cup, Nomads and British Electricity squared up to each other in front of a crowd of 1500 spectators, the largest crowd for many years. The Electricians batted first and scored 88-5 in their allotted overs, with J. Brooks scoring 21 not out and Albert Smith taking 3-27 for the Nomads. When Nomads batted, it was left to Stan Waller to hold the innings together with a score of 31. This proved to be sufficient to see the Nomads home by 5 wickets.

1947

Thirteen teams entered the league, but it was decided to have just the one league with teams playing each other only once. Dolcis set the early pace with some impressive results. Against Tite and Garfirth they scored 162, with A. Cartwright scoring 58, and then dismissed Tites for 27 with Chris Ingram taking 4-11. They followed this up with a victory over Havelock Works by 95 runs to 35, Cartwright scoring 57 not out, Arthur Lawrence taking 5-4 and Chris Ingram 4-7. Another half century by A. Cartwright saw them beat the LMS by twenty-one runs.

There were some good performances during the season. Reg Green scored 117 not out of a total of 153 against Holyoakeand Farrel scored 81 for Fuller, also against Holyoake. In the bowling department W. Chester took 7-13 against Men's Own II, Cooch and Clements took 5-17 and 5-32 respectively for Freeman Hardy and Willis against LMS.

By far the better team, however, were Dolcis and they deservedly won the championship. To cap a great season, they also reached the final of the Knock Out Cup only to lose the final by twenty-six runs to the Men's Own in front of an estimated crowd of 3,000.
Division I Batting A. Cartwright (Dolcis) Average 44.62.
Division I Dowling W. Chester (Rifles) 46 wickets at 5.58

1948

Fourteen teams entered the league and once again it was decided to have only the one Division. Last years winners of the Knock Out Cup, Nomads, entered the league for the first time, and altogether 317 players were registered. Dolcis suffered an early setback in defending their title when they were beaten by "T" Shoes, despite the efforts of Chris Ingram who took 7-27 for Dolcis. But a stubborn innings of 36 by Fred Garley saw "T" Shoes through by 74-67. Fred Smith was in good form for Fuller, taking 6-9 against Kaycee who were dismissed for 16, giving Fuller victory by 104 runs. He followed this up with 8-9, in bowling out Mens Own for 23, to record a further victory by 41 runs. Holyoake were dismissed for 24 by Dolcis, with Chris Ingram taking 8 wickets for 4 runs to enable the Bath Road side to win the match by 60 runs. Ingram was again amongst the wickets, taking 6-13 in a low scoring game against Wilson and Watson for whom J. Hawthorne also took six wickets, but Dolcis scraped home by eight runs. Albert Smith and Len Plews scored 61 not out and 53 not out respectively, as the LMS put together a score of 153-4 in their game with Rifles. The Rifles were then dismissed for 72, with S. Hills taking 6-6. Freeman Hardy and Willis were not to be out done though and they won the league by the narrowest of margins.

There was an estimated crowd of 2,000 spectators for the Semi-Final of the Knock Out Cup between Men's Own and the Town. Men's Own batted first and could only manage a score of 46, with G. Sharman taking 5-19 and D. Green taking 3-19. In reply, the Town were made to fight all the way, eventually winning by 3 wickets. It is worth noting that the Town fielded two players of first class status; H.J.H. Lamb and David Green and also another player, who would go on to have a long and distinguished career with Northamptonshire County Cricket Club, Brian Reynolds. In the final the Old Cytringanians defeated the Town. Individual honours went to:
Batting: Fred Garley (Tite & Garfirth)   Average 24.75
Bowling: Fred Smith (Fuller)   Average 3.70
Albert Smith finished second in both batting and bowling

1949
As there were sixteen teams wishing to enter the league this year it was decided to have two divisions. G. T. Whites and Wilson and Watsons were engaged in a very high scoring game. Whites batted first and scored 196-7, with Fred Garley missing a century by just eight runs. In reply, Wilson and Watsons scored 192-6, with Johnny Hawthorne making 85. The match finally ended in a draw. Ron York 4-1 and Frank Lawrence 5-10, bowling for Casuals, helped their side record an emphatic victory over Perfecta who were bowled out for 19. Division I proved to be a two horse race between The Electricians and British Railway. In fact, at the end of the season, the two teams finished up with the same number of points, and after a play-off the title went to the Electricians. Honours in the second division title race went to Wilson and Watsons who won their division comfortably.

First division batting averages were won by Reg Green of Freeman Hardy and Willis average 27.20. Les Dunmore of the Electricians took the bowling honours with 41 wickets average 3.85. The second division honours went to Johnny Hawthorne of Wilson and Watsons with a batting average of 28.9,the bowling to D.Smith with 41 wickets at 5.56 each.

Kaycee had an easy victory in the semi-final of the Knock Out Cup against Dolcis, scoring 93-9, and then bowling Dolcis out for 39, with H. Sculthorpe taking 6-22 and Eddie Armstrong 4-17. It was a different proposition in the final however when chasing a target of 101 against the Town. They could only muster 58 runs, to give the Town their first final victory in the competition since 1936.

Chapter V

1950-1959

There is a breathless hush in the close tonight,
Ten to get and the match to win,
A bumping pitch and a blinding light,
An hour to play and the last man in.

Henry Newbolt.

1950

Old Centralians made a good start to their second division campaign with a resounding victory over Nomads, who were dismissed for 36 in reply to the Cents score of 166. Walt Morris claimed 6 Nomads wickets for 16 runs.

In Division I, Joe Bent scored 103 runs for Fuller in their score of 171 for 9 declared. In reply, British Legion struggled to a score of 16-6 to earn a draw. British Railway were the next opponents of Fuller and fared no better than Nomads, with Dennis Hefford blasting a score of 89 not out, out of Fullers score of 177-2 and then bowling the Railmen out for 40. This time Joe Bent did the damage with the ball, claiming 8-6. Against Kaycee, it was the same duo that did the trick for Fuller, with Dennis Hefford scoring 67 out of a total of 125-3 dec. and then Joe Bent taking 5-18 in Kaycees score of 67 all out.

Fuller clinched the first division title when they beat Men's Own II by 20 runs, despite Dave Chaplin taking 6-17 (including a hat trick) for Men's Own. Old Centralians lost a low scoring game to Nomads by 35 runs to 31, Stan Waller doing the damage for Nomads by taking 6 Old Cents wickets for 19 runs. Cents soon overcame this setback, however, and there followed a 10 wicket victory over Tite and Garfirth. This was followed up with a resounding triumph over Perfecta by 106 runs, with Arthur Sellars scoring 104 not out and Reg Abbott taking 5-9 when Perfecta batted. Old Centralians clinched the second division championship when they defeated Nomads by 136 runs.

Individual honours went to:

Division I Batting:	A. Cartwright. (Dolcis)
Division I Bowling:	D. Chaplin (Men's Own)
Division II Batting:	L. Small (William Timpsons)
Division II Bowling:	D. Corbett (Nomads).

Wilson and Watsons and Old Cytringanians clashed in the final of the Kettering Knock Out Cup. After a keenly contested game, Old Cyts ran out winners by 5 runs. Scores were Old Cyts 75-6, with E. Corby 17 and P. Jackson 15 scoring the bulk of the runs, and H. Jarvis taking 4-26 for Wilson Watson. In reply, Wilson and Watsons scored 70 runs for the loss of 8 wickets with L. Hale scoring 37 not out.

1951

Twenty-one teams applied to join the league and it was decided to split them into three leagues: Division I and Divisions IIA and IIB.

British Electricity won the first division title despite an early setback at the beginning of the season against Casuals, who scored 158-7 declared, W. Chester scoring 85. They then dismissed the Electricians for 92, Frank Lawrence claiming 7-31. Good results followed this early reversal however, amongst them a victory over Nomads by 28 runs thanks largely to R. Groome who scored 59 and Mark Errington who took 4-24. They then won a close encounter with Dolcis by six runs, M. Errington taking 5-29. They also had an excellent result against Fuller in a high scoring game. Electricians, declared at 164-5, Eric Owen scoring 87. They then bowled Fuller out for 132, that man Errington again taking 6-60.

Havelock Works and Kaycee battled it out for the Second Division A Title, with Ray Pell in good form for Havelock Works scoring 105 in a 100 run victory over Mobbs and Lewis. He then followed this up with 8-32 against Athletic, who were beaten by two wickets. Kaycee were not to be denied however and they eventually triumphed due, in no small part, to the bowling of Eddie Armstrong who turned in some impressive performances, chiefly 7-13 against Post Office and 6-12 against Athletic.

Freeman Hardy and Willis won the other Second Division Title by playing some very good cricket, especially the one that clinched the title beating Men's Own by 120 runs (scoring 141-8 declared), and then bowling Men's Own out for 20, Reg Green taking 5-7. Other notable achievements in the league included W. Payne taking all ten wickets for twenty six runs for Fuller in their match against Casuals, and W. Chester taking seven Nomads wickets for five runs, Nomads being bowled out for ten.

Individual honours went to:

Division I. Batting.:	R. Groome (Electricians) Average 30.11.
Division I Bowling:	L. A. Dunmore Average 6.13.
Division IIA Batting:	R. Pell (Havelock Works) Average 24.36.
Division IIA Bowling:	E. Armstrong (Kaycee) Average 3.54.
Division IIB Batting:	D. Thurland (Timpsons) Average 34.60.
Division IIB Bowling:	R. Green (Freeman H and Willis) Average 4.95.

In the first semi-final of the Knock Out Cup, Teachers played GPO. Teachers batted first and put together a score of 97, with J Deer scoring 31 runs and Paul Rowney taking 4-50 for GPO. In reply, the Post Office could only make 47, N. Chambers doing the damage taking 5-24 (including a hat trick).

In the second semi-final, W.B. Wrights set the Old Centralians a target of 84-4, with Poppies favourite Tom Smith (brother of Albert) scoring 45. In reply, the Old Boys crumbled before the bowling of H. Whymant, who took 7-25 to dismiss them for 48. In the final, before an estimated crowd of 4,000, W.B.Wrights posted a more than useful score of 92, with Tom Smith and another Poppies legend, Maurice Dunkley, both scoring 20. Teachers, in reply, made a gallant attempt to get the runs (R. Dainty 23), but in the end they fell 18 runs short of their target.

1952

Once again there were three divisions and Fuller won the first division for the second time in three years, although last season's champions British Electricity pushed them very hard. Newly promoted Freeman Hardy and Willis found life difficult to begin with when they were bowled out by Fuller for 37. F. Smith took 5-13 and Gilbert Duck 5-19 (including a hat trick) to win by 57 runs. Freeman Hardys quickly recovered to record two splendid victories over British Electricity and Casuals. Terry Ingram scoring 70 in the first game and Maurice Tyrell 68 in the latter, Reg Green claiming 6-16 against Casuals.

It was a family affair for British Legion in their match against Perfecta when brothers F. Sismey and J. Sismey scored 92 and 86 respectively in Legions total of 242 for 8 declared. Perfecta were bowled out for 102. H. Smile, playing for the Post Office against Perfecta, had the misfortune to be bowled out with his score on 99. British Railway, who were the winners of Division IIB, owed much to Albert Smith. In their game with Tite and Garfirth, he scored 59 not out in an opening partnership of 143 with Harry Marlow, who scored 82 not out when they declared. Albert then went on to take 6-12 in Perfectas score of 37. Division IIA was won by Athletic.

There were some good individual performances during the season, notably 61 by Len Plews for the Railway against Timpsons, and 56 by Ray Pell for Havelock Works against Athletic. In the bowling stakes, Bert Garret 8-33 for Dolcis against Tite and Garfirth, Reg Abbott 5-16 against the Railway and Fullers Fred Smith 7-38 against Kaycee.

Individual honours went to:

Division I Batting:	N. Goodfellow (Electricians) Average 31.66.
Division I Bowling:	L. Dunmore (Electricians) Average 4.98.
Division IIA Batting:	B. Russell (Havelock Works) Average 26.00.
Division IIA Bowling:	P. Rowney (GPO) Average 4.91.
Division IIB Batting:	A. Smith (British Railway) Average 40.40.
Division IIB Bowling:	A. Smith (British Railway) Average 4.08.

In the Knock Out Cup semi-finals, the two favourites were beaten. Casuals beating the Town by eight wickets and British Railway disposing of W.B. Wrights by one run, with Albert Smith being the destroyer in chief returning figures of 7-15. British Railway were successful in the final, passing Casuals score of 84 with two overs to spare. Len Plews was the star for British Railway scoring 29 runs and taking four wickets.

1953

Fuller changed their name to Ivanhoe, which had no effect on their ability as they went on to lift the First Division title once again. Once again there would be a First Division with the Second Division being split into A and B. British Legion won the Second Division IIA Title and Staples Printers won Division IIB.

An early centurion was Charlie Richards, who scored 100 not out for Casuals in their score of 188-3 declared against LMS, who were then dismissed for 58. Ivanhoe quickly got into their stride with a comfortable four wicket win over Athletic, who were dismissed for 63, with Joe Bent claiming 6-12. This was followed up by a five-wicket victory over Freeman Hardy and Willis, who were bowled out for 57, this time the damage was done by Fred Smith who took 8-16. In their next match against Casuals, it was the batsmen who came into their own with R. Holding (42) and Roly Drew (39) being mainly responsible for their score of 174, enabling them to win the match by 100 runs. There followed a drawn game with Athletic, who, thanks to another Poppies favourite Geoff Toseland (71 not out) and Stan Waller (49), were able to declare at 145-4. In reply, Ivanhoe were 62-5 at the close. Despite this setback, Ivanhoe carried all before them and went on to win the league relatively easily.

In the second division IIA, British Legion were dismissed for 45 runs by Nomads, but in reply Nomads could only muster 26 runs, Pete Walton taking 5-33 for Nomads with R. Marlow responding with 7-10 for Legion. Marlow and Hugh Randell took five wickets apiece as Perfecta were beaten by 37 runs, with Brian Munton scoring 31 out of the Legions score of 120. Mobbs and Lewis were also beaten by 36 runs. Kaycee temporarily halted the Legions march to the Second Division IIA title when Eddie Armstrong took 6-12, dismissing Legion for 80 to give Kaycee victory by 16 runs. However, Legion kept their heads after this disappointing result to finish the season on top of the league.

Staples Printers had a truly wonderful time in Division IIB, winning eleven of their twelve matches. They didn't have it all their own way though, William Timpsons kept pace with them for most of the season. In the end, Staples proved to be too strong and went on to win the Division by four points.

Individual honours went to:

Division I. Batting: A. Sellars (Old Centralians) Average 28.40.
Division I Bowling: R. Steventon (Athletic) Average 4.78.
Division IIA Batting: P. Hawkes Average 25.60.
Division IIA Bowling: W Beasley (Nomads) Average 5.32.
Division IIB Batting: A. Lawrence (Dolcis) Average 30.62.
Division IIB Bowling: F. Neil (Staples Printers) Average 6.40.

In the first round of the Knock Out Cup, Len Plews bowling for the LMS against Tite and Garfirth had the remarkable bowling figures of 9 wickets for 10 runs, the final scores being LMS 68 Tite and Garfirth 29. Kettering Town won the competition scoring 92-4 in the final, with H.J. Potts scoring 40 not out. Their opponents were Athletic, who were bowled out for 55, with Stan Waller scoring 25 and Fillingham taking 5-32 for Town.

1954

A new competition was introduced for the coming season, the F.R. Brown trophy, which would be awarded to the best fielding side. The judging would be undertaken by the umpires, who would award points to each team at the end of each match. Freddie Brown, the Northamptonshire and England captain, donated the trophy as he felt that the players often neglected this facet of the game. The first winners were Old Centralians.

Kaycee made an encouraging start to the season with victories over Timpson and Old Centralians, with Eddie Armstrong returning figures of 6-7and 6-29 respectively. George Walklate took 7-19 in Men's Own II win over Greenlees. Whilst Dennis Thurland turned in a fine all round performance for Timpsons in their victory over the Electricians, the scores were; British Electricity 136 (R. Groome 57, D. Thurland 5-36) Timpsons 140 (D. Driver 62, D. Thurland 40 not out). Norman Cooper also starred for Staples in their win over the Railway taking 5-29 and scoring 21 runs. Old Centralians, who were runners up in the first division in 1952 and 1953, went one better this year and deservedly won the first division honours. Havelock Works, whose last success in the league was way back in 1934, when they were first division champions, had a very satisfactory season and went on to take the second division title.

In the Knock Out Cup, the Town made a good start to their campaign. They met Kaycee in the first round and restricted them to 81-8 with Adkins taking 5-28. They then knocked the runs off with out losing a wicket, with Jimmy Potts scoring 53 not out. Then in the second round they beat Athletic scoring the winning run off the last ball. Scores: Athletic 85-9 Town 88-5. In the semi-final, the Towns opponents were Old Cytringanians and after scoring 106-5 the Town looked favourite to go through, but the old Cyts dug deep and managed to get the winning run off the penultimate ball. In the other semi-final, the Teachers met Barton Seagrave and the result went in favour of the Barton team. Barton batted first in the final and put together a score of 78, (Les Dunmore 4-10 and N. Munn 6-22) then shot out the Old Cytringanians for 34, the lowest ever total in a final. It was the first time that Barton Seagrave had ever won the competition.

1955

After nine years at the helm, the league president Mr. Thomas Bird announced that he would be giving up the office. The committee reluctantly accepted his resignation and thanked him for his services to the league.

This year saw the beginning of another competition, which was to be run in conjunction with the Kettering Carnival Committee to raise money for charity. It was decided to run a Six-a-Side competition, which would be staged on a Sunday and played to a finish on that day. The winners would receive " The Edgar Towell Challenge Trophy". Little did the organisers know that this tournament would endure for the next forty years and indeed would be the most popular day in the local cricketing calendar.

There were three divisions of the league this year. Division I champions were Athletic, Division II Holyoake and Division III Dolcis. Athletics game against Freeman Hardy and Willis was a very low scoring game. Athletic dismissed their opponents for 18 with Roy Steventon taking 5-11 and Norman Pell 5-5, but in reply they lost 6 wickets in scoring the 19 runs needed, Reg Green taking 5-8 for Freeman Hardys. Athletic then went on to record easy victories in their two games with Ivanhoe and despite a defeat at the hands of Old Centralians, they went on to win the league. Ivanhoe bowled out British Railway for 7 runs, the lowest score ever recorded in the history of the league.

In Division II, despite losing to Timpsons by ten wickets, Havelock Works proved to be very consistent and were worthy champions. In Division III, Paul Rowney returned figures of 8-26 for GPO to help dismiss

Kaycee for 61, only to finish on the losing side as his team was shot out for 48. Arthur Lawrence had a good game for Dolcis against the Post Office when he scored 65 runs and then went on to take 5-47 in helping his team to a 65 run victory. Another record was also set this season when Old Centralians recorded a score of 274-6 declared against Tite and Garfirth. This was the highest score ever recorded in the league. Arthur Sellars and Geoff Mole both scored 80 and the margin of victory was 172.

In the final of the Knock Out Cup, the Town defeated Southgate by seven wickets. Scores: Southgate 101, Town 103-7, Harry Johnson scoring 43 for The Town. In the first Six-a-Side tournament Athletic beat William Timpsons in the final.

1956

The league was once again made up of three divisions with newcomers Spring Gardens joining the fold. Mr. Edgar Towell was elected to replace Mr. Thomas Bird as President.

Ivanhoe owed a lot to the Jackson brothers in their match with Holyoake. Peter scoring 51 not out in Ivanhoes score of 125 and David taking 4-15 in Holyoakes reply of 58. A feature of the match was Ray Pells bowling, he took 8 Ivanhoe wickets for 34 runs. Ivanhoe followed this up with a comfortable win against British Legion who, chasing a score of 132, could only muster 35, with Fred Smith taking 4-27. Jim Chaplin scored 33 for the winners. They did not have it all their own way though when they lost by six wickets to Casuals due, in no small part, to Nip Collyer who took 5-15 in Ivanhoes score of 77, and then went on to score 43 not out. Ivanhoe did not experience many more set backs, and went on to win the first division title. Timpsons won the second division title and Spring Gardens, in their first season in the league, triumphed in the third division. Notable individual performances during the season were: Terry Walklate 49 not out and 7-11 for Mens Own against Perfecta, Len Plews 7-11 for Railway against Casuals, Alan Gibson 5-11 for Dolcis against Nomads, Walt Beasley 6-16 for Nomads in the same match, and finally Carl Howard 9-38 against Centralians II. Ivanhoe and the Railway were the joint winners of the F. R. Brown Trophy. Old Cytringanians were the Six-a-Side champions.

The final of the Knock Out Cup was between Ivanhoe and Athletic, with victory going to Athletic. Athletic batted first and, thanks to a patient 29 not out from Stan Waller, they set Ivanhoe a target of 82 for victory. Dave Jackson played a magnificent innings of 31 not out, but it was all in vain, Ivanhoe finishing 4 runs short of their target. The Athletics fast bowler, Rory Steventon, took 4-40. An estimated crowd of 2-3,000 spectators watched the game.

1957

The league reverted back to two divisions, Athletic changed their name to Crusaders and Spring Gardens became the Foresters. Old Centralians quickly got into their stride bowling Holyoake out for 17, with John Short taking 5-11 and, despite John Hill taking 4-11for Holyoake; Cents won the match by five wickets. Crusaders were the Cents next opponents, but they offered little resistance managing to score only 44 (Reg Abbott claiming 3-11), the Old Cents winning this one by four wickets. Walt Morris took 6-5 as Railway, chasing the Old Cents target of119, were bowled out for eighteen. Ben Middleton top scored with 77. Lennie Plews took 6-38 for the Railway. Ben Middleton also starred in the narrow win of 13 runs over Ivanhoe, scoring 78 not out. Another narrow victory followed for the Cents by 1 run against Nomads, despite Nomads fast bowler Vic Tompkins returning figures of 6-28. There was no stopping Old Centralians and they had the league well and truly won before the end of the season.

In the second division, Roy Briggs of Old Centralians II scored 104 not out against Perfecta in their 116 run victory. Foresters recorded early victories over Perfecta and the Post Office and, although they did not do anything spectacular, they were consistent throughout the season and went on to finish the season as champions of Division II. Tite and Garfirth were declared the winners of the F.R. Brown Trophy.

Timpsons reached the Final of the Knockout Cup, with victories over both the Wanderers, with Dennis Thurland scoring 52 not out and Barry Maples taking 8-15, and against Old Cytringanians by seven wickets. In the final, they came up against the Town and were bowled out for 41. Dave Chaplin being the destroyer in chief taking 6-12, the Town running out winners by nine wickets. Town made it a double success by also winning the Six-a-Side tournament.

1958

The formation of the league remained the same with two divisions of ten teams in the first division and eight teams in the second. This season proved to be no different from the last one, with Old Centralians dominating the first division. They beat Timpsons by nine wickets. Timpsons were dismissed for 81 with Dennis Franklin and Pete Mann sharing the wickets and, in knocking off the required runs, Rodgers scored 58 not out. Against Nomads, they scored 132-6 declared (Colin Smith 46 not out) and then bowled out their opponents for 45 (Franklin 4-13). They carried on in this vein for most of the season and went on to make it two championships in consecutive years. Kaycee won the second division title due mainly to the bowling of Eddie Armstrong and Carl Howard, who in the three victories over Dolcis, Mobbs and Lewis and Holyoake took twenty-two wickets between them.

Other notable achievements were; Dennis Newman (Timpsons) 59 runs and 4 wickets for nine against Nomads, Barry Maples 6-9 in the same match, Dave Neal 6-7 for Ivanhoe versus Casuals, and Geoff Toseland 6-47 for Crusaders against Ivanhoe. Sadly, the Foresters were unable to fulfil their fixtures and were forced to resign from the league.

Brothers Paul and John Rowney took nine wickets between them in the semi-final of the Knock Out Cup, to dismiss Ivanhoe for 73, only to be on the losing side when in reply GPO were bowled out for 41, Len Plews taking 7-16. Southgate beat the Town in the other semi-final and then went on to win the trophy beating Ivanhoe by one run.

Crusaders won the Six-a-Side Cup for the second time in four years. Perfecta were the winners of the F. R. Brown Trophy.

1959

The league was split into two divisions, with nine teams making up each division. This year belonged to the Old Centralians. The first team won the first division for the third successive year and in so doing equalled the record set by Miss Butchers BC in the thirties of three successive championships. However, this was not the only record for the Old Cents because the second team won the second division too. No other club in the history of the league had ever produced the winners of the first and second divisions in the same season before, a truly remarkable achievement.

Alan Coles got the first team off to a good start, taking 5-8 in the eight wicket win over Casuals. This was followed by a comprehensive victory over Timpson by 100 runs with Tony Wright and Alan Coles scoring the bulk of the Cents score of 177. In their next game against Electricity, John West scored 46 runs in their total of 132 to record another comfortable victory. It was John West again with a score of 54 who sent Holyoake crashing to defeat. Casuals temporarily halted their march to the title by inflicting on the Cents their first defeat in thirty league matches dating back to 1957.

The second team began with a 49 run victory over Perfecta, with Reg Abbott taking 5-12, which helped to dismiss their opponents for 50 - Cents having been set a target of 100. N. Jessiman took 7-43 for Perfecta. This game was followed by an eight wicket defeat at the hands of GPO for whom the Rowney brothers John and Paul took 6-28 between them. Walt Morris with 6-25 and H. Sharp with 43 then guided them to a 19 run success over Barton B. Their next opponents were Tite and Garfiths and what a game it turned out to be! Batting first, the Cents were teetering on 32-5 when Maurice Tyrrell came on to bowl, and one over was all he needed. With his first ball, he bowled opener R. Chapman for 12, with his second he bowled Brian Walden for 0 and with his third ball he bowled B. Liggins for

0 to complete a memorable hat-trick, but he was not finished yet. He failed to take a wicket with his fourth ball, but he accounted for I. Jones and M. Avery with the fifth and sixth ball, to complete an over which, as a bowler, you can only dream of. The down side for Maurice was that Tites were bowled out for 21, courtesy of Pete Lord who took 7-13. Despite not displaying a high level of consistency, the second string clung on to win the league and to make it a memorable season for the Old Centralians.

Playing against Dolcis, D. Spriggs made a score of 106 for Munn and Feltons, Dave Barlow took 7 Holyoake wickets for 8 runs, Pete Munn of Barton took 7-21 as Tite and Garfirth were bowled out for 45 and Ron Ashby took 7-53 against Perfecta.

Glebe and the Town faced each other in the final of the Knock out Cup; Glebe batted first and made 71-9 in their allotted overs, with Michael Duck taking 7 Glebe wickets for 41 runs. Ray Stanley scored 43 for Town in their score of 72-1, to give them victory by nine wickets. William Timpsons won the Six-a-Side tournament.

Chapter VI

1960-1969

Hail Cricket ! glorious, manly, British game !
First of all Sports ! be first alike in fame !

James Love.

1960

Nineteen teams took part in the league and one of the founder members, Working Men's Club, successfully applied to rejoin. It was decided that there would be ten teams in the first division and nine in the second. Both leagues were rather one sided, with the Old Centralians taking the first division title with sixty points from a possible sixty four and finishing twenty two points ahead of their nearest rivals Crusaders. In winning the league, the Cents also established a record never to be surpassed, of four consecutive championships.

There were many notable performances for the Cents. Pete Mann took 6-4 including a hat-trick against Glebe, who were bowled out for 56 to enable them to take the game by eight wickets. In the sixty-six run victory over Casuals, John Short scored 56 and then took 4-33 when Casuals batted. The only defeat that they suffered was at the hands of Timpsons, who bowled the Cents out for 48, Barry Maples taking 6-19 and Dennis Newman 4-29. Timpsons lost two wickets in passing the Cents score. Working Men's also only lost one game during the season and finished twelve points ahead of Barton B to take the second division title; a very happy return to the Town League.

Paul McMillan scored 84 for Perfecta in their drawn game with Casuals. Arthur Isham scored 52 for Casuals in the same game. Geoff Toseland took 6-23 against British Legion, Brian Pell took 7-27 against Glebe and Maurice Tyrell 7-25 against Nomads. Pete Walton turned in an impressive all round display for Nomads against Barton B, scoring 53 and then taking 5-9 when Barton batted.

Old Centralians made it a hat trick of trophies when they won the F. R. Brown Fielding Trophy and the annual Six-a-Side tournament at the North Park. A truly remarkable achievement. The Knock Out Cup final was a real turn up for the book, with Southgate beating the Town by 30 runs. Southgate batted first and were dismissed for 65 runs with Dave Jackson scoring 35. When it was the Towns turn, (Dave Chaplin 5-15) and (Dave Marlow 3-17) dismissed them for 35 runs; a truly memorable victory.

1961

British Electricity, one of the founder members of the league, resigned and sadly the team was disbanded. After much discussion by the management committee, it was decided that there would be three leagues of six teams and that they would play each other three times.

Ivanhoe really set about their task in the first division, when they easily beat four time winners Old Centralians in all three games played between the sides. Twice the Cents were bowled out for 48 and they fared even worse in the third, scoring only 28. It seemed that they had no answer to the pace attack of John Gamble, Al Roberts, Dave Neal and Alan Coles. In the first game John Gamble took 9-20. Ivanhoe presented the same problems to all the other teams in the league and went through the season undefeated winning the league easily by twelve points from Crusaders.

In the second division, Working Men's started the season off in good style, with easy victories over Glebe and Barton B. This winning streak continued throughout the season. They were only beaten once all season and eventually finished sixteen points ahead of their nearest rivals, Casuals. Despite being beaten twice by the Post Office, Nomads went on to win the third division by eight points from the Post Office. They had an amazing win over Perfecta by 168 runs, Pete Walton scoring 45 with the bat and then going on to take 5 wickets for 6 runs. Holyoake, who finished bottom of the first division, claimed the unenviable record of losing all fourteen games and finishing the season without a solitary point.

Old Centralians could claim some comfort by reaching the final of the Knock Out Cup but they were shown no mercy by the Town, who won the final relatively easily. Town made 109-4, Stan Leadbetter making 78 of them, in reply Old Centralians could only muster 64 runs with Tony Wright making 20 and Nick Drake-Lee claiming 5-36 for the Town.

The final of the Six-a-Side proved to be something of an anti-climax, when Ivanhoe bowled Crusaders out for seven runs, to win the match easily.

1962

Mr. A. Johnson, the Leagues auditor, announced that he wished to stand down from the position that he had held for the past fifteen years. A presentation was made to him in recognition of his services to the League. Mr. John Short was then offered the post, which he readily accepted.

After fifteen years membership, Munn and Feltons resigned from the league due to the lack of playing members. Three new teams joined the league, Keystone Boys Club, Working Mens II and Venturers. There would again be three divisions with six teams in the first two divisions and eight in the third.

Working Men's club began their attempt at winning their third consecutive title by beating Crusaders by eight wickets, thanks largely to Martin Turner 6-12 and John Lawman 3-22. They followed this up with a ten-wicket victory over British Legion, again Turner and Lawman doing the damage with 7-15 and 3-19 respectively. In their game with Old Centralians, the Works looked like easy winners when Martin Turner took 7-31 to bowl the Cents out for 68, but in reply they could only manage a score of 38. However, they would only lose one more game and they went on to win the first division by seventeen points from Old Centralians.

Nomads went one better this season, winning the second division title after taking the third division last year. It was mainly due to their bowling that they enjoyed so much success; Pete Walton taking 7-17 in the 34 run victory over Casuals, Brian Moisey 4-8 against Cents II who were beaten by eight wickets, Ron Ashby 4-18 and Brian Moisey 3-12 in bowling Holyoake out for 41 and Ron Smith 5-27 in the win over Glebe which clinched the title by seven points. Mobbs and Lewis and Tite and Garfirth were battling it out all season for supremacy in the third division and, in fact, they finished level on points. The division was decided however, as were all the others, on a percentage basis. Tite and Garfirth came out the winners by 82.09% to 71.05%. Late in the season these two teams met each other in what was virtually a league decider. Tites bowled Mobbs and Lewis out for 13 with Terry Timms taking 6-6 to give them a nine-wicket victory.

Working Men's Club and Kettering met in the final of the Knock Out Cup and it turned out to be rather a one sided affair. Kettering bowled out the Working Men's Club for a paltry 49, with Stan Leadbetter 4-22 and John Brown 5-23 doing the damage for the Town, who then coasted home in twelve overs for the loss of only one wicket, with Stan Leadbetter scoring 27 not out. Kettering Town made it a double success when they also won the Six-a-Side tournament.

1963

Dolcis resigned from the league and there were no new applications, so the format remained the same except for division three, which would now be made up of seven teams instead of eight.

Old Centralians, after two barren years, were out to prove that they were still a force to be reckoned with, and quickly got into their stride with a ninety run win over Crusaders, with Brian Coles the star scoring 49 not out and then taking 3-14. In the vital match against Working Men's, despite John Lawman (who took 4-34 and then top scored with 47 not out), the Cents triumphed by one wicket. Next, in a surprising defeat at the hands of Nomads by eleven runs, they showed their character by going on to win the league by eight points.

Casuals and Glebe were neck and neck for the second division title. Casuals got off to a flyer, beating Mobbs and Lewis easily by eight wickets, with Jim Hales taking 5-15, and when the two teams met again Casuals dismissed the last makers for 23 to record a ten wicket victory, Jim Hales again taking five wickets, this time for 10 runs. Glebe and Casuals met in a very important game, which would probably be decisive, as far as the second division championship was concerned. Casuals batted first and declared with their score on 144-2, with Jim Hales showing his all-round qualities by scoring 77. Glebe made a tremendous effort to get the runs, Eddie Armstrong scoring 41 and Roy Shipton 35 but they were bowled out for 143 and lost the match by one run. This result tipped the scales in favour of Casuals, who took the title by three points.

In the third division, the Keystone youngsters had a fantastic season although, against Barton, it was their mentor Albert Smith who was the star, scoring an undefeated century. In the win against Perfecta, Albert took 5-29 with Barry Foster scoring 54 for the boys They then had a comfortable win over Holyoake by 45 runs, with Alan Stapleton taking 6-44 and Stapleton again with 7-45 in the win over Perfecta. Keystone did not lose a match all season and finished twelve points ahead of their nearest rivals, GPO.

Old Centralians were seeking a double success when they took on the Town in the final of the Knock Out Cup. They seemed well on course to do so, when they put together a score of 97-6 in their allotted eighteen overs with Ben Middleton scoring 26 and Roy Briggs 24. However Stan Leadbetter (59 not out) and Ray Stanley (40 not out) had other ideas and Town cruised to a comfortable ten-wicket victory.

Town also won the Six-a-Side Cup yet again, claiming another double success.

1964

After one season's absence Dolcis were welcomed back into the league. There would be eight teams in the third division and six in the two top divisions.

Working Men's Club were pitched against their arch rivals Ivanhoe early in the season and looked likely to be beaten when they were dismissed for 63, with John Gamble taking 3-14, Arnie Fox 4-14 and Al Roberts 3-15. However, a fine spell of bowling by John Lawman (5-18) saw Ivanhoe bowled out for a disappointing 33. Meanwhile, Centralians were disposing of Crusaders by 61 runs, Dick Cole scoring 49 for Cents. Ivanhoe gained revenge for their earlier defeat against the Works by beating them easily by 71 runs. Mick Ward scored 59 not out, and when the Works batted John Gamble took 7-7 to bowl them out for 38. Worse was to follow for Working Men's club when they lost by one wicket to newly promoted Casuals.

Despite these setbacks, Working Men's put together a run of seven consecutive victories to take the title by one point from Old Centralians, the percentage difference being 73.21% to 71.43%.

Timpsons, Keystone and Nomads were all in contention for the second division championship, with Timpsons eventually coming out on top. Timpsons won an important game against Keystone by four wickets - the scores: Keystone 78 (Alan Ashworth 3-18 R. Porter 3-12) Timpsons 80-6 (K. Preedy 32). Division three saw Holyoake and Dolcis scrapping it out for the title, Holyoake had some remarkable matches. Against Old Cents II, they scored 197-3 declared, with Mick Beasley scoring a magnificent 121 and Weekes 58. In reply, the Cents scored 110-6 to hold out for a draw. They then dismissed Perfecta for 18 to win the match by nine wickets, and in the return game, Perfecta were bowled out for no score. Perfecta only had six men and so set the unenviable record of recording the lowest score, and one that could never be taken away from them. Dolcis presented the next challenge. Dolcis batted first and managed a score of 114 all out. Holyoake responded well and knocked off the runs for the loss of eight wickets, Eric Dawkins taking 7-38 for Dolcis and Weekes 6-37 for Holyoake. Dolcis, however, proved to be the more consistent of the two teams and narrowly took the title by two points.

In the Knock Out Cup final, the Wanderers beat Casuals - the scores: Wanderers 95-6, Casuals 79-8. Both sides batted for eighteen overs. Crusaders won the Six-a-Side competition.

1965

It was with deep regret that the league accepted the resignation of Ivanhoe, formerly Fuller, who were founder members of the Town League. Perfecta also resigned, ending a twenty year association with the league. With eighteen teams applying for membership it was decided to revert back to two divisions with nine teams in each.

Working Men's began their defence of the title in disastrous style losing to Centralians by seven wickets, John West taking 5-19 for Cents. Cents then went on to beat Nomads by 90 runs and followed this up with an eight wicket win against Glebe, John Short returning the amazing figures of 6-2. Crusaders and Working Men's tried to keep pace with the Cents, but to no avail and the Cents went on to lift the crown comfortably. Venturers, whose rules of qualification stated a minimum age of thirty-five years, delighted everyone by winning the second division. Venturers began well beating Mobbs and Lewis by 67 runs, Joe Bent top scoring for them with 41. They then bowled out Dolcis for 50, thanks to Ron York (4-20), to win by 35 runs. Hugh Randall took 6-26 in the important game against Tite and Garfirth to restrict Tites to 99 in reply to Venturers score of 105. Dolcis were bowled out for 30 by Working Men's II, with George Short returning the creditable figures of 8-4. This was after Dolcis had restricted the Works to 60 all out. Despite losing the return match with Tite and Garfirth by two wickets and suffering a crushing defeat at the hands of Holyoake, Venturers clung on to win the league by the narrowest of margins - 1.56%, from Tite and Garfirth.

In the Knock Out Cup, there was a remarkable game in the first round when Old Centralians II were drawn to play Concord, one of the favourites to win the cup. Centralians batted first and were dismissed for a modest thirty-four runs which appeared to be a formality for Concord. However a remarkable spell of bowling by Keith Allbright, who took 8-1, completely bemused Concord and they were bowled out for 33. Evening Telegraph and the Town contested the final, with the Town running out winners by 35 runs.

Old Centralians were the winners of the Six-a-Side Cup and the winners of the F. R. Brown Fielding Trophy were Tite and Garfith.

1966

Mobbs and Lewis, who joined the league in 1913, were finding it difficult to raise a team and so regrettably they were forced tender their resignation. There would be nine teams in the first division and eight in the second. It was much more competitive this year with four teams vying for the title; Nomads, British Legion, Working Men's and Old Centralians. Nomads made a good start with a convincing win over Venturers by a huge margin of 143 runs, with Roger Pringle scoring 90 and Ron Ashby 46. When Venturers batted they were bowled out for 23, Ron Ashby taking 5-5. Working Men's started with a good win against Old Centralians. Alan Roberts took 9-25 to dismiss the Cents for 62, the Works getting home by five wickets. They followed this up with a draw against Crusaders, for whom Geoff Toseland scored 50 not out and then took 5 Works wickets for 42 runs. British Legion were bowled out for 55 by the Cents and lost the match by four wickets. By the end of the season, only five points separated the first four teams, the championship finally going to Working Men's by two points from Old Centralians.

In the second division, John Hilliard for Holyoake narrowly missed scoring a century against Barton B, when he was bowled out with his score on 96. Dolcis were in sparkling form this season; they had easy victories over Holyoake and GPO to start their campaign. They beat Glebe by seven wickets, thanks mainly to John Gamble who took 5-19, and in the return game against Holyoake, Jack Richardson scored 72 to guide them to a two run victory. Dolcis won twelve of their fourteen games and deservedly won the league by ten clear points from Glebe.

Old Centralians capped a very good year by winning the Kettering Association Knock out Cup. In the final of the Six-a-Side, Keystone Boys Club beat Glebe to win the trophy for the first time. Keystone were also adjudged to be the winners of the F. R. Brown Fielding Trophy.

1967

Reg Abbott, the chairman of the league, donated a new trophy, which would be known as the Arthur Abbott Memorial Trophy, in memory of his father. Each team would bat for a maximum of thirty overs and the team scoring the highest number of runs would be declared the winners. This season, the competition would be on a league basis and would be competed for by first division teams only. Working Men's Club resigned from the league to join the Kettering and District League and their second team also resigned, as they were unable to raise a team.

Old Centralians started with a flourish, scoring 128 against Keystone (Roy Briggs making 59 and Tony Wright 42) and then bowling the Boys Club out for 23, Tony Wright taking 8 wickets for five runs. They followed this up with a run feast against Dolcis when they scored 186. Tony Wright hitting a punishing 104 to clinch a 45 run victory. British Legion were also having a good season and they beat Crusaders by fourteen runs in a low scoring game, due to the efforts of Dave Hodson 5-7 and Brian Munton 5-21. This was followed up by a draw against the Cents. Crusaders also made a challenge for the league, but it was British Legion who eventually got home by one point from Crusaders.

Tite and Garfirth and Glebe battled it out all season for second division honours, with Tite and Garfirth finally getting home by two points. The crucial game was when Tites beat Glebe - the scores; Glebe 82 Tite and Garfirth 102-9 (P. Parker 53). Lloyd Weekes of Holyoake enjoyed a wonderful match against Old Centralians II team, when he scored 121 out of their total of 178-5, and when the Cents batted he proceeded to take 5-29 in their all out total of 47. In the game between William Timpsons and Old Centralians II, Reg Abbott scored 50 not out for the Cents in their total of 130, with Ray Patrick taking 6-35 for Timpsons. In reply, Timpsons made 65, Bill Brooks taking 7-31.

Working Men's defeated Town in the final of the Knock Out Cup by three runs. Working Men's batted first and thanks to a lightning opening stand of 49 in less than six overs by Barry Essam and Fred Beasley, they posted a score of 115. Town made a confident start, but Alan Coles broke the back of their innings when he took three wickets in one over, to leave Town four runs short at the end of their allotted eighteen overs.

The first year of the Abbott Cup saw Crusaders and British Legion share the Cup, with both teams finishing on eight points. Thirty-four teams entered the annual Six-a-Side slog, a record number of entrants. Town B were the winners, beating the Working Men's Club in the final.

1968

Tite and Garfirth resigned from the league. However an application from Taverners to enter a team was accepted by the management committee. It was decided not to continue with the F.R. Brown fielding trophy in its present form, as it proved too difficult to adjudicate. Instead a single wicket competition would be held. Second division clubs would contest the Abbott Cup this year and it would be run on a knock out basis.

British Legion made it two championships in succession, when they easily won the first division, losing only one game in the process (to Crusaders by six runs). Highlights of their season were two wins against Old Centralians, one by four wickets with Clark and Hodson claiming nine wickets between them, and in the second game coming out victors by 3 runs, despite Alan Garley taking seven Legion wickets for twenty runs. They then followed this up with two impressive victories against the talented Taverners side and went on to win the league by a clear ten points.

In a remarkable change of fortune Timpsons, who had finished bottom of the second division the previous season, took that title by seven points, with GPO finishing as runners up. Good wins against Holyoake by five runs, with Joe Bent scoring 54 and Ray Patrick taking 5-21, a four wicket victory over Barton B and an emphatic 58 run success against Keystone, put them well and truly on course to land the coveted prize. Other notable achievements were: Tony Wright 7-12 for Cents against Glebe, Keith Allbright 8-22 for Casuals against Keystone, but the star man of the season was Terry Holmes of Dolcis who dismissed all ten of the Taverners team for twenty four runs.

Individual honours went to:

Division I Batting:	R. Briggs (Old Centralians) Average 26.10.
Division I Bowling:	A. Garley (Old Centralians) Average 6.10.
Division II. Batting:	R. Baxter (Old Centralians) Average 34.50.
Division II Bowling:	K. Allbright (Casuals) Average. 4.02.

It was a repeat of last years final, when the Town met Working Men's Club. Repeat that is, except for the outcome, the Town running out winners by 15 runs. Town batted first and scored 91-7 in their allotted eighteen overs, with John Popham scoring 30 and Brian Sanders 27. Fred Beasley took 3-20 for the Working Men's. In reply, the Works could only manage to score 76-7, despite a valiant 27 from Fred Beasley.

Casuals won The Abbott Cup, defeating Venturers in the final.
Barton Seagrave were victorious in the final of the Six-a-Side tournament.

1969

After twelve years as president of the league, Mr. Edgar Towell, announced that he would be standing down this year and the meeting thanked him for his support over the years. Mr. Roy Christie was unanimously elected to fill the office vacated by Mr. Towell.

An application from the Taverners to enter their second team into the league was accepted.

Nomads only lost one league game all season, but this was not enough to stop British Legion from making it a hat-trick of championships, winning the league by a solitary point. British Legion began with a drawn game against Taverners then, thanks to John Lawman 7-14; they beat Glebe by fifty runs. Lawman did even better against Crusaders, taking 8-4 to ease Legion home by 67 runs. Meanwhile, Nomads put together some good results notably the game with Old Centalians when, having been set a target of 164, they eased home by 6 wickets with Terry Lewis scoring 80. Legion and Nomads met for what proved to be the deciding game, and it was Legion who triumphed, with Ken Gully 79 and Carl Howard 41 guiding them to a total of 155-7 declared. In reply, Nomads could only muster 37.

Dolcis were so dominant in the second division that they had the league well and truly won long before the season ended. The winning margin being a massive seventeen points. The highlight of their season was the victory against Barton when Eric Dawkins took a hat-trick in his spell of 4-14.

Individual honours went to:

Division I. Batting:	J. West (Old Cents) & Ken Gully (British Legion) Average 38.00.
Division I Bowling:	J. Lawman (British Legion) Average 4.67.
Division II. Batting:	K. Preedy (Dolcis) Average 35.50.
Division II Bowling:	T. Holmes (Dolcis) Average. 4.09.

Taverners beat the Nomads in the final of the Abbott Cup, and in the Six-a-Side it was Taverners who once again came out on top.
Town and Crusaders fought out an exciting game in the final of the Knock Out Cup the tie going down to the last ball, which ended in favour of the Town by one run.

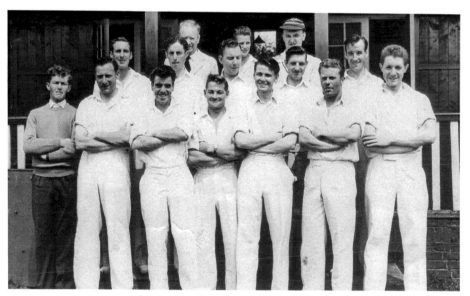

Old Centralians: Town League Champions 1957
Back Row (l to r): R Braithwaite, R. Chamberlain, R. Abbott
Centre: J. West, J. Short, N. Oldham, D. Franklin, C. Smith
Front Row: A. Godsen, D. Cole, B. Middleton, H. Rodgers, P. Cox, A. Wright

Foresters: Town League Division II Champions 1957
Back Row (l to r): Landlord - Robin Hood, H. Maycock, M. Hill, J. Mobbs,
R. Prentice, G. Short, K. Mobbs, D Clarke, T. Hyman
Front Row: D. Short, J. Foster, P. Curchin, J. Winkle, R. Wyldes,
T. Ingram, T. Dawkins

Working Mens Club: Winners of the Kettering Association Knock Out Cup 1967
Back Row (l to r): F. Beasley, B. Essam, A. Roberts, A. Coles,
R. Wyldes, J. Lawman
Front Row: A. Stapleton, D. Short, R. Poulson, B. Isham, B. Foster

Athletic: Town League Division II A Champions 1952 - Celebration Dinner
Back Row (l to r): R. Bonner, B. Ashby, B. Deaken, J. Morgan, I. Wolacott, B.
Goldsworthy, R. Prentice, T. Sinclair, S. Sayles, L. Ginns
Front Row: L. Lewin, L. Chester, Not Known, R. Steventon, V. Broderick, L. Garry, T. Austin

Kaycee: Division II A Champions 1951
Back Row (l to r): D. Dunkley, R. Tarry, J. Hollis, F. Fualkner,
E. Armstrong, C. Groome
Front Row: R. Shaw, D. Underwood, A. Johnson, A. Chapman, V. Bickley

Albert Cartwright and Chris Ingram going out to open the batting for Dolcis 1948

Old Centralians toasting Mr. R. Braithwaite in celebration of the club's 40th anniversary held on 3rd October 1978.
Pictured left to right: Tony Wright, Peter Mann, Mr. R. Braithwaite, Colin Smith, John West and Peter Lord.

Tudors: Abbott Cup winners 1988
Back Row (l to r): B Walden (Umpire), M Wittering, Pete Daniels, J. Pringle, M. Rolfe, B. Davis G. Beasley (Umpire)
Front Row: M. Beasley, P. Gamble, T. Gamble, A. Kirk, J. Warwick

Arnie Fox (left) and Tony Driver going out to open the innings for Athletic in the 1956 Knock Out Cup Final. Athletic were the winners

British Legion: Town League Champions 1967, 68, 69
Back Row (l to r): D. Randall, V. Clark, B. Miller, T. Norton, B. Hudson,
K. Gully, J. Taylor
Front Row: L. Rowney, D. Hodson, J. Lawman, B. Munton, H. Randall, K. Evans

William Timpsons: Division II Champions 1956
Back Row (l to r): D. Thurland, D. Porter, A. Ashworth, K. Preedy,
J. Russell, R. Patrick, A. Tilley
Front Row: M. Briggs, J. Welch, B. Maples, T. Essam, E. Westley. Scorer in front

E. C. Gravestock

Ground: Northampton Road

Secretary:

W. R. WADE, 17 School Lane

Date	Club	Ground	Result
May 13	Mobbs & Lewis	...	h
20	Freeman, Hardy & Willis	...	h
27	Mobbs & Lewis	...	a
June 3	Kaycee	...	a
10	St. Mary's	...	h
13-14	Kaycee	...	h
17	Miss Butcher's	...	a
24	Northampton (True Form)	...	a
27-28	Havelock Works	...	h
July 1	Wilson & Watson	...	a
4-5	T. Bird & Sons	...	a
8			
11-12	Wilson & Watson	...	h
15	Northampton (True Form)	...	h
22	Havelock Works	...	a
29	Freeman, Hardy & Willis	...	a
Aug. 19	T. Bird & Sons	...	h
26	St. Mary's	...	a
Sept. 2	Miss Butcher's	...	h

26

Wilson & Watson, Ltd. 1st XI.

Ground: The Grange

Secretary:

F. BAMBRIDGE, 27 Cornwall Road

Date	Club	Ground	Result
May 6	Freeman, Hardy & Willis	...	h
13	T. Bird & Sons	...	a
20	St. Mary's	...	h
27	Freeman, Hardy & Willis	...	a
29	Woodford	...	a
June 3	Havelock Works	...	h
6-7	Miss Butcher's	...	h
10	Faire Bros., Leicester	...	h
13-14	Gravestocks	...	a
17	T. Bird & Sons	...	h
24			
July 1	Gravestocks	...	h
8	Castle Ashby	...	a
11-12	Mobbs & Lewis	...	a
15	Mobbs & Lewis	...	h
22	Kaycee	...	h
29	Miss Butcher's	...	a
Aug. 19	Kaycee	...	a
26	Havelock Works	...	h
Sept. 2	St. Mary's	...	h

27

Two pages taken from the 1927 Handbook

Chapter VII

Memories of matches lost and won,
Of summer afternoons and sun,
Of many a doughty innings played,
Of catches missed and catches made.

Alfred Cochrane.

1970

A new club, Four Seasons, successfully applied to join the league. This
brought the number of clubs in the league to seventeen, so Dolcis and Barton
B were promoted to bring the first division up to nine teams. The single
wicket competition was discontinued after only two seasons.

Last years champions, British Legion, made an impressive start,
beating Glebe by the huge margin of 176 runs, Ken Gully scoring 73. But in
their next outing against Crusaders they fell to the bowling of Brian Pell (6-
13), to lose the game by seven wickets. Crusaders, in turn, also lost by seven
wickets to Taverners, and in the return game Taverners repeated the margin
of victory. British Legion meanwhile were beating the Post Office by 88
runs, John Lawman 62 and Brian Munton 62 getting the bulk of the runs,
and Dave Hodson taking 6 Post Office wickets for 13 runs. Crusaders,
British Legion and Taverners battled it out for the title and although
Taverners lost two fewer games than Crusaders, it was Crusaders who won
the league by four points.

In the second division, it was Casuals who set the early pace with
wins over Venturers by 21 runs, (Rex Walpole taking 5-36) and Four
Seasons by 46 runs, this time it was Keith Allbright with 7-23 who did the
damage for Casuals. This was followed up by a 46 run win over Keystone,
Richard Dexter claiming 5-22. Casuals capitalized on their good start to
take the title by nine points from Taverners II.

Individual honours went to:

Division I Batting:	B. Foster (Taverners) Average 65.00.
Division I Bowling:	J. Lawman (British Legion) Average 6.67.
Division II Batting:	R. Bailey (Venturers) Average 28.80.
Division II Bowling:	R. Smith (Timpsons) Average 4.90.

Town defeated Taverners in the final of the Knock Out Cup. British Legion
finally won the Six-a-Side competition at their sixteenth attempt. British

Legion failed in their attempt to add the Abbott Cup to their trophy cabinet, when Old Centralians beat them in the final.

1971

There were two resignations from the league, British Legion who joined the District League and Glebe, who were sadly unable to raise a team for the coming season. Glebe, formerly Kaycee, had first joined the league in 1935. William Timpsons cricket club changed their name to Tite and Garfirth, to fall in line with a take-over between the two companies. Newly formed Argyll was admitted into the league, which meant that there would be two divisions with eight teams in each. There would be a new competition this season called the Roy Christie Cup. All matches would be played on the same day and all matches would be played at the North Park. Each team would bowl a maximum of ten overs and each bowler allowed to bowl only one over. The tournament was to be run on a knock out basis, until there was an eventual winner. Taverners went one better this season going through the season undefeated and reversing the roles on last years champions Crusaders, by finishing four points ahead of them to become champions for the first time.

In the second division, Holyoake started the season very well with a comfortable win against Venturers by four wickets, and they followed that up with an eighty run success against Taverners II, who they bowled out for eight, Carl Howard taking 6-4. Joe Bent of Tite and Garfirth had a game to remember. He scored 101 not out of their total of 167 for 4 declared. In the Taveners reply of 100 he took 4-19 (including a hat trick). Despite losing to Keystone by six wickets, Holyoake finally clinched the second division title, when they beat the Argyll by 120 runs. The scores were: Holyoake 175-5 (D P. Nicholson 53) Argyll 54 all out (J. Hilliard 7-7).

Individual honours went to:

Division I. Batting: B. Foster (Taverners) Average 37.50.
Division I Bowling: A. Garley (Taverners) Average 5.39.
Division II. Batting: D. Watts (Holyoake) Average 29.80.
Division II Bowling: J. Hilliard (Holyoake) Average 6.23.

Taverners and Town again contested the Final of the Knock Out cup and again it was Town who came out on top, taking just eleven overs and two balls to score the 62 runs required for victory. There was some consolation for Taverners, when they lifted the Six-a-Side Trophy and they also won the Abbott Cup. Taverners made it a hat trick of wins, when they became the first winners of the Roy Christie Cup.

1972

Due to the lack of playing memberss, the Post Office, who had been members of the Town League since 1951, tendered their resignation.

Taverners dominated the league and again won the championship with very little opposition. They proved to be too strong in all departments of the game and at the finish they ran out easy winners. In the second division, Tite and Garfirth enjoyed a very successful season and maintained consistency throughout to emerge as champions.

Individual honours went to:

Division I Batting:	T. Lewis (Taverners) Average. 38.80.
Division I Bowling:	K. Allbright (Casuals) Average 5.90.
Division II. Batting:	L. Gee (Venturers) Average 29.80.
Division II Bowling:	M. Chapman (Tite and Garfirth) Average 7.60

At the leagues Annual Meeting, a proposition was made that the league should adopt a limited overs format and, interestingly, the proposal was defeated.

In the semi-finals of the Knock Out cup, Taverners beat Working Mens Club and in the other game Town beat Dolcis by the narrowest of margins, one run. It was third time lucky for the Taverners, who beat Town in the final, restricting the County League side to 69 in their eighteen overs and then knocking the runs off for the loss of 4 wickets, Weekes scoring 38 not out. Christie Colts won the final of the Six-a-Side. Taverners won the Abbott Cup for the third time in the last four years.

1973

Taverners resigned from the league in order to join the District league, however their second eleven would remain in the league. Nomads were also forced to resign due to lack of members. Christie Colts were accepted into the league and Dolcis changed their name to B.S.F.C.C., whilst Tite and Garfirth changed their name to Tudors. Casuals, who were celebrating the twenty-fifth anniversary of the formation of the club, really did it in grand style by winning the championship for the very first time. It was a proud moment for Frank Lawrence, one of the club's longest serving members. The title was clinched in grand style against BSFCC, Casuals winning the match by 122 runs. The scores were: Casuals 144-7(Richard Dexter 88) BSFCC 22 (Keith Allbright 6-9 and Rex Walpole 4-9).

Wellingborough Indians were the winners of division two and they began with a 64 run victory over Christie Colts, with Manhar Desai taking 3-4 and Navendra Patel 3-4 in the Colts score of 36. They then repeated the win in the return match by 57 runs, with Navendra scoring 59 runs for the Indians and Navaje taking 6-24, as the Colts were dismissed for 63. They then clinched the league with a five-wicket win over Taveners II. 1973 will be longed remembered by Shashi Dholakia who, when playing for Centralians II, took all ten Christie Colts wickets for fourteen runs.

Taverners reached the final of the Knock Out Cup for the fourth successive year. They made it two consecutive wins when they were comfortable winners over Great Oakley. Taverners also won the Six-a-Side Cup by defeating Loddington in the final by four runs. Wellingborough Indians were the winners of the Abbott Cup.

1974

Mr. Harry Coe resigned as secretary of the Kettering Cricket Association after holding the office for forty-three years. Harry was the main reason why the Knock Out Cup was such a successful and popular competition. Because of him, many hundreds of pounds were raised for charity and local cricket owed him a great debt of gratitude for his unceasing efforts on its behalf. Harry always carried out his duties in an efficient and cheerful manner and in recognition of his services, at the next meeting, the President of the Kettering club presented Harry with a silver salver and a transistor radio. Casuals II applied to join the league and were readily accepted. There would be two Divisions; the first division would comprise of six teams with eight teams making up the second division.

Old Centralians turned the clock back by taking the first division title, their first success since 1965. The secret blend was a mixture of youth and experience, with old hands like Colin Smith, Tony Wright and John West, joining forces with the likes of Ian Briggs, Roy Baxter and Tony Curchin. Early victories over Casuals II by two wickets, and Christie Colts by five wickets, saw Taverners II attain an early supremacy in the second division. They did not falter and deservedly went on to win the league.

Southgate and the Town met in the final of the Knock Out Cup. Southgate batted first and managed to score 69-7 in their eighteen overs. The Town passed this total for the loss of two wickets, with Gerry Sands scoring 41. In the Abbott Cup, Old Centralians met Crusaders in the final, with victory going to the Cents, to complete a very satisfactory season. In the Six-a-Side, the Town won the competition for the fifth time. Taverners defeated the Presidents XI to win the Roy Chistie Cup.

1975

Old Centralians I resigned from the league in order to join the District League, Casuals II also resigned. Because of the dwindling numbers there was only enough teams to run one division this season. Crusaders set the early pace, with a four wicket success over Holyoak. The scores were: Holyoake 105 (John Hill 37 not out, Barry Maples 3-6), Crusaders 108-6. In their next match Crusaders disposed of Wellinborough Indians by 68 runs, Terry Holmes 5-29 and Dennis Newman 4-34 bowling the Indians out for 77. When Simbas played Crusaders, they were no match for them either, being bowled out for 67 and losing the match by nine wickets. Old Cents II suffered the same margin of defeat when they met Crusaders. Crusaders carried on in this vein for most of the season and were inevitably crowned champions at the end of the season.

Barton easily beat Rushton in the first semi-final of the Knock Out Cup and Taverners defeated the Town in the other semi-final. This set up an interesting final between the two District League rivals. The outcome was disappointing however, with Barton being bowled out for 58 and Taverners getting the runs for the loss of one wicket, with Weekes scoring 31 not out. It was new boys Brixworth against old boys Taverners in the final of the Six-a-Side, but reputations counted for nothing as Brixworth ran out comfortable winners. In the Abbott Cup, it was Crusaders again who took the honours, defeating Casuals in the final. Unlucky Casuals were also beaten in the final of the Roy Christie Cup.

1976

Last years champions, Crusaders, were not giving up their title easily and they made a determined start to the season with a six wicket victory over Jumbos. The scores were: Jumbos 55 (Eric Dawkin 4-20 and John Gamble 3-9) being the chief destroyers, Crusaders 56 (Osborn 27). They then had a convincing win against Tudors with Barry Maples and John Gamble posting fifties in their score of 153-3 and Terry Holmes taking 6-20 in Tudors reply of 49. Holyoake scored 135-9 in their first game against Crusaders, with Ron Dolby scoring 32 and Terry Holmes, again amongst the wickets, with 5-35. But an innings of 44 from Mick Ward saw Crusaders home by four wickets. In the return fixture, Terry Holmes had another five-wicket haul and this time the margin of victory was 88 runs. Crusaders were in irrepressible form and really there was no one able to challenge them. They took the title for the second year in succession.

Great Oakley and Isham contested the final of the Knock Out Cup. Oakley set Isham a target of 89, thanks largely to J. Oram (34) and J. Bielby (36), but in reply Isham managed only 59, their score not being helped by four of their batsmen being run out. Simbas were the winners of the Abbott Cup. Once again it was Taververs who won the Roy Christie Trophy, by defeating Wellingborough Indians in the final. It was an all Taverners affair in the Six-a-Side with both the first and second teams reaching the final. In a closely contested game, the first team managed to sneak a victory off the last ball of the match.

1977

Once again, it was Crusaders who set the pace. They sent Flamingos packing by bowling them out for 54, (Terry Holmes taking 7-20) and they then knocked the runs off, for the loss of two wickets. It was Holmes again, this time taking 8-2 (including a hat trick) against Jumbos to shoot them out for 44. This was in reply to Crusaders score of 155-9, Brian Osborn scoring 42. Cruasaders season followed the pattern of the previous two and they became the fourth team to have won the league in three consecutive seasons.

Isham once again reached the final of the Knock Out Cup; their opponents this time were the Town. Town batted first and Isham did well to restrict them to 84 - Dick Tilley top scoring with 29. But once again Ishams batting let them down and they were bowled out for 65. Champions Crusaders completed the double when they won the Abbott Cup to add to their league title. In the Six-a-Side tournament and the Roy Christie Trophy, Taverners retained both trophies.

1978

Holyoake were bowled out for 25 by Crusaders with Holmes and Gamble taking four wickets each for the champions, enabling them to stroll home by nine wickets. Crusaders then disposed of Centralians II by four wickets, to stake their claim to emulating Old Centralians I in winning four consecutive titles. They received a set back however, suffering only their second league defeat in four seasons, when they were beaten by Venturers. Venturers scored 140 due, in part, to Brian Bambridge 58 and Phil Boyden 40. In reply, Crusaders were bowled out for 118. Crusaders were never the same team after this defeat and lost the form that had carried them to three championships. Tudors took full advantage of the Crusaders demise and put together some good results, with wins over Jumbos by seventy seven runs (Mick Chapman taking 4-15) in Jumbos score of 67, and a sixty run success over Weetabix, Mick Chapman again amongst the wickets with 5-17 in the Weetabix score of 78. Other good results followed and they clinched the title when they beat Holyoake by fifty-seven runs.

There were some fine individual performances during the season notably Rick Cooper 6-6 for Christies Colts against Holyoake, John Hill 4-18 including a hat-trick for Holyoake against Centralians II, D. Halsey 70 for Weetabix against Cents II and finally Steve Walton who turned in a fine all round performance in scoring 90 and then taking 5-12 for Christie Colts against Venturers.

It was another case of unlucky Isham, when they reached the final of the Knock Out Cup for the third year running, only to lose to the Town once again. The scores were: Isham 87-5, Town 89 (Dave Ingham 39 Brian Saunders 29). Crusaders and Jumbos shared the Abbott Cup, after finishing level on the same number of points. Taverners won the Roy Christie Trophy for the third year in succession (this would be the last season that this Trophy would be competed for). In the Six-a-Side, Casuals thwarted Taverners efforts to make it three wins in succession, when they beat them in the final.

1979

Limited overs cricket was introduced into the Town League for the very first time. Discussions had first taken place in 1972, so careful considerations had been made before the move was finally undertaken. The matches would consist of thirty-six overs.

Tudors, last seasons champions, made a disastrous start to the season losing by five wickets to Crusaders and by one run to Weetabix. Crusaders, after their victory against Tudors, followed this up with a win against Jumbos, with Dave Gilbert scoring 36 runs and taking 4-25. In their next match against Centralians II, they rattled up a score of 209-7, the run makers being Dave Gilbert 74, Barry Maples 57 not out and Gordon Livesy 54. Crusaders were unable to maintain their early season form and Jumbos took full advantage with a consistent run of good results from mid-season onwards; the highlights being a 37 run win over Christie Colts and a conclusive victory against Weetabix, whom they beat by 110 runs. B. Tailor scored 43 for Jumbos and when Weetabix batted, A. Joshi and Dilip Patel both took 3-6. Jumbos consistency paid off and they went on to win the title for the very first time. Gordon Livesy of Crusaders was elected as Player of the Year and the young Player of the Year was Steve Walton.

Played on the Town ground, before a crowd of approximately one hundred spectators, Great Oakley and the Town clashed in the final of the Knock Out Cup. The game turned out to be the highest scoring final since the competition began. Town batted first and thanks to Mike Dilley, who scored 61, they scored 146-5 in their allotted eighteen overs. Oakley made a valiant attempt to get the runs, but were all out with their score on 124, Dave Ingham being the most successful bowler for Town taking 3-4. Jumbos were seeking to add the Abbott Cup to their League title but Tudors had other ideas and easily beat them in the final. Barton Seagrave A beat Taverners B in the final of the Six-a-Side.

Chapter VIII

1980-1989

As in life so in death lies a bat of renown,
Slain by a lorry (three ton) ;
His innings is over, his bat is laid down :
To the end a poor judge of a run.

George Mcwilliam.

1980

With only nine teams entering the league, it was once again decided to have just the one division. Crusaders made a good start to the season, beating Old Centralians II by seven wickets, with Dave Gilbert scoring 89 out of their total of 126-3. They followed this up with a 23 run success over Flamingos, with Gordon Livesy scoring 44 and then taking 5-25. Christie Colts also made an excellent start against Venturers, scoring 203-7, with Ian Starsmore scoring 86 and C. Hawkins 60. They then bowled Venturers out for 15 (Kelly Meagan 6-8 and Ian Hodgson 4-6 doing the damage). Their next opponents were Kangos and, thanks to the father and son combination of Pete and Steve Walton (who scored 43 not out and 49 not out respectively), they won by six wickets. In the crunch game against Crusaders, the Colts bowled Crusaders out for 95, Cooper taking 3-14, and the Colts passed this total for the loss of only 6 wickets. Tudors and Old Centralians II then felt the full force of Rick Coopers bowling, (he returned figures of 7-30 against Tudors and 7-30 against Old Cents) which gave the Colts two easy victories and eventually the championship. The player of the year award went to Rick Cooper and the young player of the year award went to Steve Walton, both of Christie Colts.

Oakley were hoping to stop Kettering from lifting the Knock Out Cup for the fourth consecutive year, but their hopes were dashed when they could only muster an all out score of 69, which Town passed for the loss of five wickets. Jumbos were the winners of the Abbott Cup. Weekly and Warkton played Barton Seagrave in the final of the Six-a-Side, with victory going to Weekly and Warkton. A total of two hundred and two pounds, a record for the event, was raised for charity.

1981

Champions, Christie Colts, opened their campaign with a drawn game against Tudors, with Rick Cooper scoring 46 and Osborne 59 in their total of 163-8. But they could not get the last three Tudor wickets as they closed on 90-7. Despite amassing the highest score ever recorded in the Town

63

League, 292-5, with fifties from Cooper, Meagan and Wade, they had to settle for another draw against Harlequins, who were 62-7 at the close (Cooper 4-6 and Meagan 3-9). Brentmere were their next opponents, whom they beat by 176 runs, with Meagan and Cooper scoring half centuries and then taking 5 wickets each as Brentmere were bowled out for 33. Meanwhile, Tudors were going about their business in a less flamboyant way, and they were putting together some good results to keep in touch with the Colts, hoping that they would slip up in the race for the title. Slip up they did, when according to a report in the Evening Telegraph, five of the Colts players decided not to finish the season but to play football instead. This decision had disastrous effects for the Colts who were soundly beaten by Old Cents II, followed by a three run defeat at the hands of Crusaders and finally succumbing to Tudors by 172 runs, which meant that Tudors took the title. Dennis Newman, the Crusaders opening bowler, made it a season to remember when he captured all ten Kango wickets for fifty runs, as the Indian side were bowled out for 93. Player of the year was John Warwick of Tudors and the young player of the year was Kelly Meagan.

Kettering and Oakley again contested the final of the Knock Out Cup and the result was the same as the previous season, with the Town making it five consecutive wins. Tudors made it a double celebration when they added the Abbott Cup to their League success. Barton Seagrave reached the final of the Six-a-Side, but their attempts to win the trophy, as they did in 1980, were dashed by Brixworth.

1982

Twelve teams entered the league this season, the only new club being Juventus. It was decided to have a first and second division with six clubs in each. Brian Bambridge of Venturers scored 98 in their total of 179-7 against Christie Colts, and then Douggie Bellamy took eight Colts wickets for just eight runs, as they were bowled out for 39. Colts also suffered at the hands of Holyoake, for whom Ron Dolby and Bill Ashby scored fifties in a total of 158-8 and Ian Mason claimed 7-25, as the Colts were shot out for 59. However, it was Tudors who set the pace in the first division. Warwick and Glanfield notched half centuries in their one hundred run victory over Kangos. They followed this with a twenty run win over Juventus, which was a bowlers match with Rick Cooper taking 7-30 for Juventus and Roy Smith claiming 6-17 for Tudors. There followed victories over Flamingos and Jumbos. In the return match with Flamingos, Malc Briggs had quite an extraordinary match. Not only did he score 53 runs in Tudors total of 164-3 (Malc was the club wicket keeper!), as a last gasp effort, he took off his pads and gloves and proceeded to bowl his leg breaks with devastating effect, returning figures of 7-32. This win guaranteed Tudors the title for the second successive year.   Old Centralians took the second division championship. They clinched the title with two emphatic wins over Harlequin by eight wickets (Pete Mann taking 7-10 in the Harlequin total of 39) and then against Christie Colts they amassed a score of 174-7 (R. Berwick 51 Ron Ashby 34).   They then bowled their opponents out for 65, with Ron Ashby taking 7-29.

Once again the Town reached the final of the Knock Out Cup, but this time they came undone against Isham. Chasing Ishams score of 86, Town could only muster a disappointing 56. Jumbos were the winners of the Abbott Cup. Brixworth won the annual Six-a-Side tournament to record their second win in successive seasons.

1983

Juventus resigned from the league after only one season, but Tudors entered their second team in the competition, so the format remained the same with two divisions. Tudors were again champions and so became the fifth team to win three titles consecutively. Tudors clinched the title in a remarkable match. Flamingos, with Manher Patel taking 5-9 (including a hat trick) bowled them out for 75.   In reply, Flamingos collapsed to 63 all out, with Roy Smith taking 3-1. Tudors owed much to the bowling of Mick Chapman, Roy Smith and Dick Strangeward for their successes over the three years and the team thoroughly deserved the accolades accorded to them.

In the second division, Christie Colts had a good win over Holyoake with Terry Flak taking 9-27 in Holyoake's score of 66. This after the Colts had set them a target of 93, with Tim Osborn making 41 and Bill Ashby taking 7-14 for Holyoake. Successive victories over Old Cents II and Tudors II, set Kangos up to challenge for the honours, and in a crucial match against Christie Colts, they scored 276-8 with Prakash Jami making 103 not out. They then bowled the Colts out for 69, to win their first Town League title. Crusaders again had a bowler who took all ten wickets in a match, this time it was Rex Walpole, who took 10-49 against Christie Colts. Kettering Town failed to reach the final of the Knock Out Cup for the first time in seven years. This season Weekly and Warkton met Oakley in the final, with Weekly coming out on top. Tudors once again completed the double when they won the Abbott Cup. Juventus and Wellinborough Indians contested the final of the Six-a-Side, with Juventus the victors.

1984

Mercenaries applied to join the league and their application was accepted. This meant that there would be six teams in division one and seven in division two. Tudors began the defence of their title in fine style with victories over Crusaders and Old Cents II, and in the return game with Old

Cents it was a personal triumph for Mick Chapman, who took 4-8, (including a hat trick). Meanwhile, Jumbos, despite an early setback against Flamingos, proved to be the most consistent team in the league and they deservedly took the title. New boys Mercenaries, set a hot pace in the second division. They beat Brentmere by eight wickets, with Billy Payne taking 5-28, as Brentmere were dismissed for 63. It was Payne again (with 6-36) doing the damage against Harlequin, who were beaten by four wickets. Mercenaries clinched the title when they dismissed Venturers for 63, to run out easy winners.

For some reason, it was decided not to run the Knock Out Cup this year. Flamingos were this seasons winners of the Abbott Cup. It was an all Weekly and Warkton affair in the Six-a-Side competition. Both their first and second teams reached the final. Rather surprisingly, it was the second team who came out on top, due in no small part to K. Watts, who achieved a hat trick for the second string.

1985

Old Centralians II, Tudor II and Jumbos all resigned from the league, which was offset, a little, by Wellingborough Indians rejoining; they also entered a second team as well. There was to be one division this season. Wellingborough Indians returned with avengeance and in their first match they beat Venturers by 112 runs, with Gulah Mohamad scoring 37 in their score of 202. Sitaram Patel had a good game for Kangos against Brentmere, taking 6-17 and then scoring 30 of the 50 runs that they needed for victory. Mercenaries and Wellingborough Indians featured in a high scoring drawn game. Mercenaries made 206-6 (Redding 79, Payne 59) and in reply Indians made 167-5 (Kanshik Joshi 90 not out). Barry Maples scored a half-century in Crusaders 66 run victory over Tudors. Easy wins over Melton and Harlequin and a narrow victory against Tudors, sent Mercenaries to the top of the table, where they remained for the rest of the season to become champions.

This season saw the last Knock Out Cup competition played under the auspices of the Kettering Cricket Association. Oakley and Kettering met in the final of the Knock Out Cup and victory went to Oakley. They ran out easy winners by nine wickets. The scores were: Kettering 77-6 and in reply Oakley scored 78-1 with Ian Althorpe scoring 42 not out. Wellingborough Indians celebrated their return to the League by winning the Abbott Cup. Old Taverners won the Six-a-Side by beating their old adversaries, Crusaders, in the final. Highlight of the first round was a Mickie Ostle hat trick for Taverners against Barton Seagrave.

1986

Wellingborough Indians II withdrew from the league, leaving just ten teams to challenge for honours. There were also two other significant resignations from the league this year. Mr. Reg Abbott who had been Chairman of the league for the past twenty-two years and Mr. John Hill, who had been secretary/treasurer since 1969, decided to step down. Paul Rowney was elected as secretary and Eric Dawkins took on the role of chairman.

David Beale of Holyoake became another centurion, when he scored exactly 100 in Holyoake's score of 138-7. This was in reply to Flamingos score of 195, for whom Biran scored 80. Neil Mobbs of Melton also scored a century when he notched 102 against Harlequin who were beaten by 122 runs, with John Pike dismissing six Harlequin batsmen for ten runs. Father and son Bill and Paul Mcdowell scored 52 not out and 43 respectively, in Brentmeres score of 159-7. When their opponents Flamingos batted, young Paul took 5-9. Holyoake and Wellingborough Indians were neck and neck for the title for a long while. Late victories over Crusaders and, more importantly, Holyoake saw the Indians needing to beat Harlequin to win the league. They accomplished this with very little trouble scoring 190, thanks to Jitu Patel 69 and Umesh Patel 58, and then bowled Harlequin out for 48.

Crusaders won the Abbott Cup. In the final of the Six-a-Side Holyoake defeated Juventus to win the competition for the first time.

1987

Wellingborough Indians made a good start in defence of their title, with a comfortable six-wicket win against Crusaders. However, Harlequin unexpectedly beat them by 59 runs. The man mainly responsible was Steve Bailey, who scored 39 and then took 6-36 when the Indians batted. This defeat only served to make the Wellingborough team more determined than ever, and successive victories over Crusaders, (by six wickets) and Kangos (by two wickets) put them back on the right track to retain their title. Three centuries were scored during the season, with two of them going to Steve Bailey of Harlequin. The first, 121 against Brentmere, and the second, 120 against Venturers. Ken Gully was the other centurion scoring exactly 100 against Venturers. Pete Gamble of Tudors took 7-11 against Melton, (including a hat trick) clean bowling the last three batsmen. Crusaders bowled Melton out for 38 and the Holmes duo of father Terry and son David took 5 wickets each.

Flamingos were the winners of the Abbott Cup. The Six-a-Side tournament was won by Overstone.

1988

Nine teams took part in the league and three of these teams found sponsors and subsequently changed their names; Harlequin became Bletsoe Transport, Brentmere became Ram Sports and Melton changed to Red Lion Broughton. Holyoake carried all before them this season and were worthy and popular champions. Amongst their many victories on the way to the title were a five wicket victory over Kangos, another five wicket win over Venturers with Steve Ashby taking 6-18 in the Venturers score of 68, and David Beale scoring 48 for Holyoake. They then managed to scrape home by one wicket against Flamingos thanks to Steve Ashby again who took 5-24. Holyoake clinched the league title when they defeated Tudors by eight wickets. Steve Kendall of Ram Sports scored 102 in his team's total of 162-9 against Venturers. Steve Brock the Red Lion bowler turned in the remarkable figures of 9-17 as Red Lion dismissed Venturers for 41. Steve Kendall of Ram Sports was voted the player of the year for 1988.

It was Tudors again in the Abbott Cup capturing the Trophy for the fourth time. Overstone followed last year's success in the Six-a-Side, when they lifted the cup again this year.

1989

Flamingos and Red Lion Broughton left the league but, fortunately, two new clubs applied to join and were accepted. Saracens and Mill Road kept the number of teams at nine.

Ketan Patel scored 103 for Kangos in their score of 173-6 against Holyoake. Steve Kendall for Ram Sports, and Dave Fenwick for Crusaders, both scored 76 for their respective clubs in the game between Ram Sports (who scored 145-8) and Crusaders (147-7). Steve Kendall was in the runs again for Ram Sports, scoring 84 in the drawn game against Saracens. There were two hat tricks during the season, Dick Strangeward for Bletsoe in their win against Venturers, (finishing with final figures of 6-23) and Ketan Patel for Kangos against Bletsoe. His efforts were to no avail though as Kangos were beaten by 96 runs.

Saracens, a very young side, were making quite a mark in their first season in the league. They opened their account with a 41 run victory over Bletsoe, thanks mainly to Russ Steventon, who was the elder statesman of the team, taking 6-25. They then disposed of Holyoake by 56 runs, again Russ Steventon taking 6-25. Then, in a close game with Crusaders, they came out on top by 19 runs. Although it was not all plain sailing, the youngsters hung in there well and at the end of the season they had a superb 60 run win over Crusaders to clinch the title.

Bletsoe were this years winners of the Abbott Cup. Mikado won the Six-a-Side tournament.

Chapter IX

1990-1993

Nor sweeter music in the world is found
Than that upon an English Cricket ground.
R. Radcliffe Ellis.

1990

Once again nine teams entered the league and this season would throw up
some remarkable individual performances, with no fewer than seven
centuries being recorded during the season. Peter Daniel of Tudors scored
102 not out against Saracens, Mark Mason scored 144 not out in Ram Sports
score of 219-5, also against Saracens, Roger Fox scored exactly 100 for
Bletsoe in their score of 224-2. John Kemp of Ram Sports scored 91
against Saracens and then followed this up with 105 not out against Mill
Road. Mark Wittering of Tudors made a score of 104 against the luckless
Saracens. Dave Fenwick of Crusaders scored 125 against Mill Road and he
bettered this score when Crusaders met Saracens with a score of 133. There
were some good bowling performances as well. Richard Downing took 5
wickets without conceding a run for Mill Road against Saracens, Mick
Goodhall took 7-27 for Venturers against Ram Sports, Terry Flak took 5-1
for Bletsoe against Ram Sports and Paul Eaton returned figures of 6-46,
(including a hat-trick) for Ram Sports against Saracens.

Last years champions, Saracens, were a much-changed team this
term and quite often fielded teams with a high proportion of 15-year-olds in
their line-up. Worthy winners of the league, however, were Bletsoe, who
swept all before them and won most of their matches in convincing style.

Bletsoe, last years winners of the Abbott Cup, retained the trophy
this year to add to their League title. They narrowly missed out on doing the
treble, when they reached the final of the Six-a-Side, only to lose out to
Wellingborough I.C.S.

1991

Mill Road entered their second team in the league to bring the number of
teams up to ten. Crusaders began their campaign well with a hat trick of
victories over Mill Road II, Holyoake and Ram Sports. Saracens youngsters
also made an encouraging start after last seasons disappointing effort, when
they thrashed Mill Road II by 154 runs, with Tim Burton scoring 86 not out
and Sean Stokes taking 8 wickets for 4 runs for the boys. John Warwick
scored 107 for Tudors against Mill Road II, Dean Pridmore notched 112 not
out also against Mill Road II and Steve Bailey of Bletsoe scored 103 runs

69

against Saracens. Crusaders were in a rich vein of form and they clinched the title with an exceptional game against Bletsoe. Bletsoe batted first and managed a total of 122, with Dean Maples taking 4-22 for Crusaders. In reply, Crusaders scored 123-9, to scrape home by the narrowest of margins. Jack Myrick scored 46 runs to hold the Crusaders innings together and Steve Bailey took 6-39 for Bletsoe. There were many notable performances during the season; David Holmes of Crusaders who scored 59 runs against Mill Road and then proceeded to take 7-31 (including a hat trick) when Mill Road batted. Goodall and Hanby took five wickets each for Venturers as they bowled Mill Road II out for just 11 runs. In the match between Mill Road I and Mill Road II, Brock took 8 first team wickets for 28 runs, all to no avail though, as the first team ran out winners by 129 runs to 97.

Tudors won the Abbott Cup for the fifth time, when they beat Holyoake in the final. Holyoake made them fight all the way and they did not concede victory until the final ball of the game. Kangos and Wellingborough Indians faced each other in the first ever all Indian final in the Six-a-Side. Kangos batted first and could only manage a very disappointing total of 21; a score which provided no difficulties to Wellingborough Indians who cruised home to an easy victory.

1992

Eight teams entered the league and they were: Bletsoe, Venturers, Foresters, Ram Sports, Crusaders, Tudors, East Carlton and Saracens. Sadly, Holyoake who first joined the league in 1931, under the name of Havelock Works, found it necessary to resign their membership. Bletsoe and Crusaders were fighting neck and neck for the championship all season. Bletsoe began their campaign with a 21 run victory over Venturers, despite Mick Goodall taking 6 Bletsoe wickets for 17 runs. Meanwhile, Dave Fenwick of Crusaders thrashed the East Carlton bowling, scoring 96 out of their total of 198-6. David Holmes then took 7-21 in East Carltons reply of 77. Crusaders drew their next match with Tudors, for whom Mick Chapman and Keith Wright batted out the last ten overs to earn the draw. Bletsoe took advantage of Crusaders slip up by beating Saracens by 137 runs and they followed this up with a win over Foresters. Bletsoe then surprisingly lost to Venturers by 89 runs to 64 due mainly to Alan Coles, who scored 45 of the Venturers runs, and to Mick Goodhall, who took 6-20 when Bletsoe batted. Crusaders looked to be favourites for the title, when they crushed Bletsoe by 75 runs, thanks to Dave Fenwick who scored 63 runs and to Holmes who sent 7 Bletsoe batsmen packing for 18 runs. Crusaders, however, seemed to lose their way after such an important victory and they allowed Blesoe to overtake them. The season finished with Bletsoe winning the league.

Bletsoe also went on to win the Abbott Cup to end a very successful season for them. Centralians and Mikado met each other in the final of the Six-a-Side, and in a very high scoring game Mikado ran out winners by 69 runs to 41.

1993

Only six teams entered the league and it was to prove a very good year for the Crusaders. They went through the year losing only one game and deservedly winning the league. They started off drawing their first game against Foresters in a high scoring affair. Crusaders posted a score of 213-8, with David Holmes making 73 and Dean Maples 83. But Foresters hung on at 128-9 with Geoff Vowden, the former Poppies manager, scoring 48. There followed easy wins against Midlanders and Tudors and an exciting game against Foresters. Foresters batted first and scored 154-8, with Thornton scoring 73. In reply, Crusaders scored 156-6, with Chris Fulcher making 83 not out. There followed a drawn game against Tudors. In reply to Crusaders 184-5 (Fulcher 55 and Weekes 62 not out), Tudors reached 113-3, Beale making 53. In the third meeting between the teams, Crusaders won a closely fought game scoring 192-7, Chris Fulcher made 89 in reply to Tudors score of 188-4, with John Warwick 61 not out and Daniels 52 not out. Despite unexpectedly losing to Saracens by 126 runs to 77, the Crusaders went on to lift the trophy by beating Venturers by 77 runs. Mark Wittering of Tudors hit 150 against Venturers, the highest recorded innings in Town League history. However, the record was equalled, when Mark Hanby of Venturers hit 150 against Foresters.

In the Abbott Cup, Crusaders carried on where they had left off in the League, to go through to a comfortable win over Tudors in the final. In the final of the Six-a-Side, Wellingborough Indians beat Crusaders and so thwarted Crusaders, in their attempts to lift their third trophy of the season.

The Annual General Meeting of the league was held at the beginning of November. The secretary reported that only four teams had indicated that they would be joining the league – these were Crusaders, Saracens, Tudors and Foresters. The league secretary, Mr. Paul Rowney, was asked to contact the Kettering & District League with a view to amalgamating the two leagues for the coming season. After some consideration, the District League turned down this proposal, but stated that places would be offered to any Town League sides wishing to join them for next season (three teams actually took this offer up).

The Town League was now left with very little choice, and a reluctant decision was taken to disband the League.

So the final curtain came down on a league that had spanned nine generations of cricketers and given so much pleasure to so many people.

To perpetuate the Town League, the Abbott Cup would replace the District League's Knockout Cup, and the Albert Smith Memorial Trophy would be played between the Premier League Champions and the Rest of the League.

Paul Rowney was elected on to the executive committee and would be responsible for the running of the Roy Christie six a side charity competition. The competition only survived for one more season – Liitle Harrowden were the winners.

Chapter X

The players of my time.

The erring ball, amazing to be told!
Slipped through his outstretched hand and mocked his hold
James Love.

My first experience of Town League cricket, dates back to 1950 when, as a 15 year old, I went to work for Freeman Hardy and Willis in Mill Road. Freeman Hardy were a very successful Town League side and I was only too happy to join them. You were expected to go to net practice twice a week, if you didn't go, then you were not considered for selection. If I was lucky I would be selected as twelfth man, and in those days if the game finished early they would carry on playing in order to give every one a game, including the twelfth man. Reg Green was the star player for us. He was a very hard-hitting batsman and if he got himself set, it meant a lot of hard work for the fielding side. He bowled at medium pace and he used to get the ball to zip off the wicket. Batsmen found him to be quite a handful. In the field he was very fast and very few balls got past him. Reg was certainly one of best allrounders that I ever saw in the Town League.

Lennie Coe was a brilliant batsman and he loved to play the cut shot - he was quite a useful bowler as well! Harold Chapman was the captain and he was also a very good bowler. The Hope brothers, Dennis and Horace, also played for us, Claude Wildman was the wicket-keeper and the character of the team and he kept us in fits of laughter with his witty remarks.

Dolcis were a team to be reckoned with and they had a fast bowler by the name of Chris Ingram who, to a fifteen-year-old, seemed quite fearsome. He would come charging in at you with his jet black hair flowing in the wind, which made him look even more formidable. Their batting was also very strong and in Arthur Lawrence they had a batsman who always seemed to have plenty of time to play his shots. Eric Dawkins played for Dolcis when they changed to the BSFCC and then later when they amalgamated with Crusader. He continued to play until 1990, and even after this, if they were a player short, he would turn out for the club. He was a wonderful club man and a fine cricketer too. Eric was a more than useful opening bowler. He bowled left arm around or over the wicket to great effect and when he was batting he liked nothing better than throwing the bat at the ball.

Les Dunmore and Mark Errington were prolific bowlers for the Electricity and they carried the brunt of the bowling for many years.

The batting was left in the capable hands of Eric Owen, Norman Goodfellow and Reg Groome.

Havelock Works were indeed fortunate to have the services of one of the best allrounders in the league in Ray Pell. He was an outstanding batsman who scored a lot of runs, and he was quite an accomplished bowler as well, turning in many a match winning performance. Sometime later along came another great allrounder in Lloyd Weekes who was a tremendous batsman and opening bowler, he could also turn his hand to bowling spinners if the need arose, he was a genuine allrounder.

Other players to make their mark for Havelock Works, or Holyoake as it became known, were Bill Ashby and his son Steve who were both very good bowlers, John and Dick Hilliard (both allrounders), John Hill who was quite a stylish batsman and a useful change bowler and Mick Beasley who was an excellent batsman. Talking of Holyoake brings to mind the occasion, when the Hilliard brothers Dick and John were playing for them against Crusaders. Crusaders bowler Terry Holmes struck Dick a very painful blow on the leg. So badly was he incapacitated that he had to be taken to the hospital. He underwent some precautionary tests and the leg, was found to be badly bruised, but nothing was broken and he was discharged. As he was about to leave hospital he spotted his brother in the out patients department and when he asked him what he was doing there, John told him that he had been hit on the foot whilst batting, by the same bowler, Terry Holmes. Terry obviously believed in keeping it in the Hilliard family.

Frank Lawrence and Frank Neal of the Casuals were a perennial pair and wherever the Casuals played a match they were always the first two names pencilled in. Frank Lawrence was a very fine allrounder, and it would be nice to know what his final tally of runs and wickets was when he decided to call it a day. Incidentally, Frank never wore a pair of gloves when he batted, and I can not remember him ever being hit on the hands. Ron York was a founder member of the Casuals, and he was a very useful left arm bowler who took many wickets. Charlie Richards was a very good batsman for Casuals, indeed he was good enough to have scored a century in the League. But the star of the team, had to be Keith Allbright who was a fine bowler, and I think it would be fair to say that he was very highly regarded as a batsman as well. Jim Hales was an allrounder of quality and a tough competitor. Rex Walpole was another allrounder who always gave 100%.

Brothers Ken and John Mobbs were well known footballers in the Kettering area, their skills did not end there though, because they were both very good cricketers. They both played regularly for the Spring Gardens (Foresters) and they were the backbone of the batting. Alan Broadbent, Bob Clark and Pat Brookes further complemented the batting line up.

74

Pete Curchin, another well-known amateur footballer, was the Spring Gardens wicket keeper. The capable pair of John Foster and John Winkle spearheaded the bowling.

Crusaders, who were previously the Athletic, had what was arguably one of the most lethal pair of fast bowlers in the league in Roy Steventon and Norman Pell. Norman was the more accurate of the two and Roy was, arguably, the faster, but they complemented each other very well and they were quite a handful. When they retired there was no let up for the batsman because along came another bowler who was somewhat fiery, Brian Pell. Mention the name Brian Pell to most cricketers and they would have visions of this giant of a man thundering in towards the wicket and unleashing a hand grenade with all the ferocity that he could summon. He bowled left arm and you always had to be on your guard when facing him. He carried the brunt of the bowling for Crusaders at this time.

Talking of Brian Pell reminds me of the Crusaders wicket keeper Derek Plews who was a really energetic player throwing himself all over the place. But as good a keeper as he was, it is not this I remember him for, because Derek was Brian Pells biggest fan. If Brian bowled a good length ball Derek would bellow down the wicket "WELL BOWLED BRIAN", if he bowled a rank long hop he would bellow down the wicket "WELL BOWLED BRIAN", if he bowled a full toss he would bellow down the wicket "WELL BOWLED BRIAN". Derek was a great character and he was certainly an inspiration to Brian, not that he needed it.

Geoff Toseland also played for Crusaders, and he was a fine allrounder, he only bowled medium pace but he was so accurate that you could not take any liberties with him at all. His batting, like his bowling, was not flambouyant, but he played some quite delicate shots, he guided the ball here, he guided the ball there, and before you knew where you were he had scored thirty or forty runs.

Crusaders were a good side and they also had some very useful batsmen indeed in Mick Ward, Tony Driver and Brian Osborn, to name a few. But for me the classiest batsman of them all was Stan Waller. Everything that he did on the cricket field he did with style, he was an imposing man, a tall man, who stood very erect and his driving was right out of the top draw, he was a very good bowler too.

My old school captain, Brian Munton, played many years for British Legion and also captained them. Brian was a very good allrounder who bowled medium pace, and was a hard hitting batsman who on his day could score a lot of runs quickly, he was also a brilliant fielder. Bob Miller used to open the batting for the Legion and he was very difficult to get out when his mind was made up to stay there. Jack Taylor was quite an accomplished wicket keeper for the Legion, and he was also a more than useful batsman. David Hodson joined the club as a boy, and he quickly developed into a very good allrounder. He bowled fast medium and he was so accurate for some one of his age. His batting took more time to develop but as time went by he became far more proficient, and he soon gained a reputation as one of the best allrounders in the League.

Finally, a mention for one other cricketer, Ken Gully. A favourite with Poppies fans for his goal scoring feats, Ken was a truly remarkable batsman with zero respect for bowlers. If the ball was there to be hit, he hit it hard, and he played many a match winning innings for the Legion. Keith Preedy, who joined the Legion from Tite and Garfirth, had a rather unusual experience when fielding against Old Centralians. The game was played on the Centralians wicket at Northampton Road. This ground adjacent to some common land, which was home to the Fair that visited Kettering annually during the first week in July - Kettering Feast Week. One of the Old Centralians batsmen hit the ball out of the field and it finished up amongst the caravans and the various rides in the field next door. Keith went trotting after the ball and he seemed to be gone rather a long time. The fielding side were about to go and look for him when he was seen emerging out of the fair ground attractions. What can only be described as hilarious, but not to Keith, was the fact that his trousers were hanging down in shreds and he had several claw like marks on his legs. It turned out that an over zealous alsation had been guarding his masters property which just happened to be where the ball came to rest, needless to say the chuckles continued long into the game, with Keith eventually joining in.

When you hear the name GPO, you immediately think of the Rowney brothers, John and Paul. For so long they were an integral part of the Post Office cricket team. Indeed, there are some who thought they were the team, well the bowling anyhow. They both opened the bowling, John bowling left arm medium pace, Paul was right handed and bowled just that little bit faster, but they complemented each other very well. Paul was also a very good hitter, and he would crouch, leaning on his bat waiting to dispatch the ball out of the ground. Kevin Mann was also a very good medium pace bowler for the Post Office.

Eddie Armstrong was a bowler who seemed to take wickets at will, he turned in some very impressive figures for Kaycee, or Glebe, as they later became. Carl Howard also played for Glebe and he was a very good allrounder. He was a very correct batsman and was very difficult to get out when he was in one of his more belligerent moods, he was also a more than useful seamer, who displayed great determination - a worthy opponent indeed! Other players who played for Glebe and come to mind are Dave Dunkley, Ron Tarry, Bob Darlow, Roy Shipton and Bernard Brown; all of them were good cricketers.

There were many fine cricketers who played for Ivanhoe and they had what was probably the finest bowling attack that was ever assembled in the Town League - the batting was pretty good too. Alan Roberts and John Gamble opened the bowling. Alan Roberts was about six foot five inches tall so he brought the ball down from a great height. As a consequence, he managed to get a lot of lift off the wicket and he bowled fast as well, he was a very difficult customer indeed. John Gamble was a compact bowler. He had a beautiful action and he was very fast, yet he always seemed to bowl well within himself. I personally rated him as one of the best bowlers in the league. They were supported by Dave Neale and Alan Coles who were both very good seam bowlers in their own right, and just to add a little variety, they had Arnie Fox to come on with his slow tempting leg-breaks which often caused the batsmen to relax a little which was their ultimate undoing.

Dick Tilley, Dave Jackson and Peter Jackson were the front runners in the batting stakes for Ivanhoe, and they were among the very best in the league. Alan Coles was a hard-hitting batsman, and in Arnie Fox they had a batsman whose concentration was amazing. If I had to pick someone to bat for my life it would be Arnie Fox. I remember the time Arnie Fox went on holiday to Cornwall, whilst playing for the Works. He was so keen not to miss a game that he insisted that he would be back in time to play on the Saturday. Well, he left Cornwall at the crack of dawn and drove non stop all the way home. He managed to get there in time to open the batting, and for all of his trouble he was out to the very first ball of the innings!

I worked for Mobbs and Lewis for a few years, so I got to know some of their players quite well. Gordon Aldwinkle was one of the mainstays of their team and he played for them for a quite a few years. He was a more than useful bowler and if he survived the first few overs he could lay into the best bowling attacks. Brothers Derek and Trevor Bryant were both very capable batsmen, and other players who were assets to the team were Roger Mobbs and Jimmie Capps. But the man who really shone for them was Roger Pridmore, a left-handed batsman with a very good eye. He scored a lot of runs for Mobbs and Lewis and if he had taken the game more seriously, he could have been one of the best batsmen in the league.

John Short was a truly magnificent allrounder. To bat against John was the most difficult experience that I ever encountered. He was an off break bowler but he bowled them at medium pace and he could turn the ball two feet. He would sometimes have as many as five men around the bat, and they would all be situated on the leg side, and when the wicket had a bit of bite in it he was unplayable. He was also a very good batsman, both stylish and aggressive, and Centralians were lucky to have a player of his calibre in their side. Centralians had a host of good players in their ranks, Pete (Tufty) Mann was one of the best opening bowlers in the league and he seemed to take wickets every week. Dick Cole, Colin Smith, Ben Middleton, Geoff and Dennis Mole, Roy and Ian Briggs were all capable of making big scores and Arthur Sellars, Walter Morris, John West, Tony Wright, Brian Coles, Roy Baxter and Brian and Alan Garley were all very good allrounders. You do not win the league seven times in eleven years without having good players. But, by the same token, you have to keep those players motivated and focused and their two captains during their most successful period, Reg Abbott and Dennis Franklin, did this admirably.

My old friend Norman Cooper who played for Nomads was a very useful allrounder, and so was Pete Walton who, when he bowled, seemed to generate a lot of pace off the pitch. Lennie Culmer, who was a very good wicket keeper, could also bat a little as well, and Ron Ashby was a bowler with a classic action who could generate both pace and lift off the pitch. He was also handy with the bat and if he had concentrated more on his batting, he would have been an allrounder to be feared. The Lewis brothers also played for Nomads; Tony, Derek and Terry were all very good batsmen and they accounted for a good many of the Nomads runs.

Lennie Plews, (the brother of Derek who was mentioned earlier) played for the Railway, and in my opinion was the finest seam bowler of his generation. He had pace and he could move the ball either way, and he never seemed to have an off day. I can remember matches when he has taken teams on virtually single handed and given a good account of himself. When he put his mind to it he was also a very good batsman. Albert Smith also played for the Railway and he was an allrounder of sheer quality. He bowled seam and later turned to bowling big off breaks. He was also a batsman of some substance, good enough to have scored a century when he had turned fifty. Alberts career spanned some five generations. Harry Marlow, Lubby Loasby and Arthur Isham also played for the Railway. Whilst we are on the subject of the Railway, I remember my brother telling me of the time when he was playing against the Railway. The match was being played at Northampton Road and the Railway won the toss and batted first. They got off to a very good start scoring forty runs with out losing a wicket. It was at this stage that the captain threw the ball to my brother and asked him to have a bowl. The batsman played the first two balls carefully and off the third ball he went for an extravagant cut. There was a loud noise as the ball sailed though to the wicket keeper and every body appealed for a catch behind the wicket. The umpire thought about it for a moment and then said "NOT OUT, but if he does it again he will be!"

Barry Foster, John Sellars, Alan Garley, Mickie Ostle and Len Rowney all played for the Taverners who dominated the Town League in the seventies. Barry Foster was their most dominating influence, he was a resolute batsman who could attack when the situation called for it and defend when the need arose, he was also a useful medium paced bowler. Terry Lewis, Mickie Ostle and Lloyd Weekes accounted for most of the batting and in Alan Garley, John Sellars and Lloyd Weekes they had a very formidable bowling attack. If this was not enough they had, in Len Rowney, one of the best wicket keepers in the league.

When Barry Maples played for Timpsons he was, in my opinion, one of the finest allrounders in the league, he bowled extremely fast and he was very accurate. He seemed to be able to bowl yorkers at will, and it was not unusual for him to bowl as many as four in the one over. His batting was dynamic and he was a tremendous hitter of a cricket ball. Many a time he has lifted the ball out of the ground across the road into the premises of Timpsons factory. Time took account of his bowling, and I think a shoulder problem caused him to give up this facet of the game. Perhaps this also made him more cautious when batting, because he lost his cavalier approach to the game and he would be intent on making sure that you did not get him out. He was still a very effective cricketer but I preferred Barry when he was lifting the ball out of the ground.

Another very good cricketer for Timpsons was Dennis Thurland, a real competitor, who would never give in until the last ball had been bowled. Dennis was the captain of Timpson for many years and he was also their opening batsman. He never gave his wicket away cheaply, and I would put him amongst the very best of opening batsmen in the league. Ray Patrick was a very good bowler for Timpsons and he took a large amount of wickets for them. Other notable players for Timpsons were Edgar Westly and Alan Ashworth.

It is not unusual to find two brothers playing for the same team, but to find four, well that is something else. That is just what Tite and Garfirths had in the Preedy brothers; Ken, Keith, Daz and the eldest one Don, who was the father figure. They were all pretty good cricketers and they were all accomplished batsmen. I still remember walking along Bath Road with Ken Preedy - I think at that time he played for Crusaders and their opponents that day were Tudors, who I happened to be playing for. We were idly chatting about this and that when Ken spotted a dapper little figure about fifty feet in front of us, he was an umpire and Ken, on spotting him, groaned "Oh no, I hope he is not umpiring our game, he always gives me out LBW no matter whether I am in front or not." Soon we arrived at the ground and the game got under way, Crusaders made a good start and the two openers, one of whom was Ken, had put on about forty runs or so when the captain tossed the ball to me and asked me to have a bowl. Ken was facing and I bowled the first ball to him which struck him on the pad, and I was convinced that it struck him in line with the middle stump, I let out an ear shattering appeal to the umpire, who just happened to be the same umpire that Ken and I had spotted in the street as we walked to the ground. Without a moments hesitation he raised his finger to give Ken out. As he trudged dejectedly back to the pavilion he made a point of coming over to me and whispering some very choice words into my ears.

Tite and Garfirth also had another trio of players playing for them who were brothers; Barry, Alan and John Cartwright, who were the sons of Albert Cartwright, one of the leagues finest batsmen. Other good cricketers in their team were; Don Wright, who opened the batting for them, and I remember they had a really fast bowler in Terry Timms, who unfortunately left the club to move to Northampton. Brian Summerly was another bowler who was not particularly fast but he was a bustling type of a bowler. Then there was Maurice Tyrrell who was one of the few spinners in the league, he bowled off – breaks to great effect. He was also quite an accomplished batsman.

Roy Smith and Mick Chapman were two bowlers who played for Tudors, and for as long as I can remember, while Tudors had a team those two opened the bowling for them. Mick was a very accurate bowler whilst Roy relied more on his speed; a very good combination. John Warwick, Phil Cross and Brian Isham were the mainstay in the batting department and they were ably supported by wicket keeper Malc Briggs.

Venturers were a team of golden oldies and it is my one regret that I never had the chance to witness some of their players in their prime. Players such as such as Joe Bent, Jim Chaplin, Gilbert Duck, Walt Beasley, John Hawthorne and Jimmie Prescott. Having said all of that, I saw enough of them to realise that they were all good cricketers and they must have been something to watch when they were in their prime.

John Lawman and Martin Turner were a bowling force to be reckoned with, Martin bowled left arm round the wicket, was very fast and a real handful for any batsman. John was the ideal foil for Martin, he bowled orthodox right arm over the wicket, he was not quite as fast as Martin but he was very accurate. Indeed and these two spear headed the Working Mens attack. Alan Coles, George Short, Fred Beasley and Barry Essam bowled medium pace with George Short turning to spin if the need arose. There were many useful performers such as Stuart Moore (a very good allrounder), Alan Reed, Mick Jenkinson, Phil Traynor, Murray Hume and Terry Gilham who were all excellent club men. The main batting was left in the capable hands of Barry Essam, Pat Brookes, Bob Clark, John Lawman, Fred Beasley, Alan Coles and Bob Wyldes.

Freddie Roughton who played for Perfecta was a very stylish opening batsman, and I think it would be fair to say that he carried the batting hopes of the team on his shoulders. Another Perfecta batsman who was a good player was Paul McMillan, who was an extremely aggressive batsman; if you did not get him out early in his innings he would make you pay dearly for it. Other useful performers for them were Gordon Beeby and Lennie Hope.

These then are the players of my time, and the players I remember. Some I may have forgotten and for this I apologise, although it was not intentional. For me it has been a great pleasure remembering all these players. What is rather surprising is that as each name comes to mind you remember something about them, some little thing that they perhaps did in a match. Maybe they dropped a catch, maybe they held a catch, perhaps they made the winning hit, perhaps you bowled them out, or perhaps they bowled you out.

British Electricity: Town League Champions 1949
Back Row (l to r): D. Brown, R. Windsor, N. Goodfellow, Not Known, L. Dunmore
Front Row: R. Stapleton, Not Known, K. Ball, Reg Groome

Freeman Hardy and Willis: Town League Champions 1948
Back Row (l to r): Not Known, A. Worley, N. Oldham, C. Foster,
H. Chapman, E. Cooch, Umpire
Front Row: T. Jones, B.Clements, Reg Green, C. Wildman, M. Tyrell

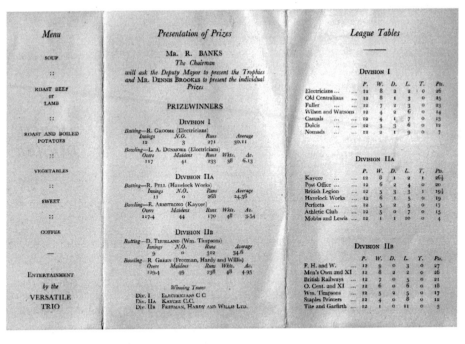

Annual Dinner Menu 1951- depicting prize winners

Shasikant Dholakia's remarkable feat of taking all ten wickets for Old Centralians II against Christie Colts (reported by the Evening Telegraph).

Crusaders beaten by Town in the 1969 KO Final
Back Row (l to r): B. Osborn, B. Pell, G. Toseland, O. Dalziel, B. Maples,
R. Pridmore, M. Ward, D. Plews
Front Row: R. Christie, D. Lenton, Brackwell, N. Beale

Kettering Town League Representative side, selected to play the Champions (Havelock
Works) 1934. Portrays two of the finest batsmen in the
league's history: A. Cartwright with pads on,
and Fred Garley - back row, second player from the right.

Ivanhoe pictured in the late1950's
Back Row (l to r): D. Turner, B. Underwood, M. Ward, D. Jackson,
S. Moore, Jack Chaplin
Front Row: Jim Chaplin, J. Bent, P. Jackson, G. Duck, J. Hawthorne

G. Starmer (left), F. Garley (centre) and A. Lawrence of Thomas Birds
are caught on camera before the game

Derek Plews and Mick Ward walk out to open the batting for Crusaders against the Town in the 1969 Knock Out Final.

Wilson and Watsons Cricket Club circa 1946

Argyll who joined the League in 1972
Back Row (l to r): R. Downing, R. Smethers, T. Hearn, B. Garley,
N. Franklyn, D. Randall, T. Collins
Front Row: B. Short, A. Ferguson, J. Holmes, N. Thomas

Dressed for the occasion: A charity cricket match at Barton Seagrave.

Chapter XI.

People

In Cricket, as spectators know,
There is one unwritten law,
Whatever way a batsmans out,
He is never leg before!

L. B. Wilson

This chapter is devoted to the people who made it possible for so many people to be able to play Town League cricket for a period of some nine decades. All of them gave their time unselfishly in the running of the league. Some of them gave financial help and most of them had good administration skills, which were used in the efficient running of the League. One person in particular was responsible for introducing more youngsters into the Town League than any other man in its eighty-two years history. These men all made a difference, they gave their time freely and all the cricketers that have ever played Town League cricket owe them a debt of gratitude for the manner in which they carried out their duties on behalf of the League. There is one other group of men, sometimes much maligned; who deserve a mention and that is, of course, the umpires.

Mr. Charles Saunders

Charles Saunders was the first president of the Town League, taking up the office in 1912 and continuing in the post until his death on the 16th June 1944.

Mr. Saunders was born in 1859 in High Wycombe. He later moved to Kettering where he went into partnership with Mr. J. H. Gotch to form the well known firm of architects Messsrs Gotch and Saunders. Mr. Saunders, at one time, was captain of the Northants Club and Ground, and he was still on the playing staff well into his seventies. He was also a member of the Northants County CC. Mr. Saunders used to love to put up a set of stumps on the Gas House field, off Northfield Avenue, place sixpence on the middle stump and get local lads and youths to bowl at him. Every time the sixpence was knocked off the middle stump, the proud bowler would claim it as his own.

He was a keen sportsman and it was he, together with Dr. Allison, who were founder members of Kettering Golf Club, he became the club captain in 1898. He was elected president in 1943 and 1944. Such was his appetite for the game that he managed to play two rounds of golf in a day when he was in his eighty fourth year. He never took any task on unless he could give it his undivided attention, and the Kettering Town Cricket league was no exception. He attended most of the dinners and he also attended some of the meetings. He was extremely good to the league and he would, more often than not, donate all of the trophies. When the news of his death broke, the Evening Telegraph printed a tribute to him. Kindness, generosity, outspokenness and fearlessness, were widely recognised characteristics of this grand old man.

Mr. Thomas Bird.

Mr. Thomas Bird was invited to become the president of the league in 1946, and he held the office until 1955. He was born in 1886 and his childhood was spent in Kettering. He briefly moved to Northampton to take up the position of improver in the shoe industry to enable him to learn the trade. When he had served his apprenticeship, he returned to Kettering to work for his father. Mr. Bird became chairman of Dolcis, who were one of the biggest shoe manufacturers in the town. He became a leading figure in the shoe industry, and he was awarded an MBE in recognition of his services throughout the Second World War in connection with British and American services footwear.

Although there is no evidence of him playing cricket, or indeed, ever having a great love for the game, Mr. Bird was a staunch supporter of the Town League and would willingly give of his time if he thought that he could make a difference. He attended many of the league presentation dinners and he was always generous in making donations towards trophies. At the age of 65 he announced his retirement from Dolcis; although he did carry on with his duties with the British Footwear Federation. Mr. Bird sadly died in 1957 at the age of 71.

Mr. Edgar F. Towell.

Mr. Towell was born in Kettering in 1901 and he set up a thriving footwear company, which was situated in Stamford Road, in Kettering. He was a well-respected businessman and he was considered to be a fair and honest employer.

Mr. Towell had a passion for cricket and he excelled in this field, so much so that he was good enough to be selected for the County side. He spent ten years with the County, but owing to his business commitments, he was unable to play on a regular basis. He scored nearly 1200 runs at an average of 12: 75, with a top score of 66 made against Essex at Kettering. But bowling was his main forte and he took 102 wickets in his first class career. Mr. Towell also played for Kettering Cricket Club and he quite often turned out in some of the Kettering Cricket Association Knock Out matches. Brian Reynolds, who had such a successful career with the County scoring nearly 20,000 runs for them, was a protégé of Mr Towell, and it was he who introduced him to the County Club.

Mr. Towell was elected to the office of president in 1956 and he held the post until he announced his retirement in 1969. He made many donations to the Town League and he also gave a cup for the Six-a-Side tournament, which was known as The Edgar Towell Challenge Trophy. Mr. Towell passed away in 1972 at the age of 71.

Mr. Roy Christie.

Roy Christie was president of the league from 1969 until it was disbanded in 1993. He was very good to the league and his sponsorship ran into many hundreds of pounds. He also sponsored a team of young lads, some as young as twelve or thirteen, who were being brought together by Albert Smith. These young lads did not have any proper equipment, Roy was approached and he agreed to buy all the kit that they would need. Henceforth the team became known as Christies Colts.

Mr. Christie was born in 1926 in Ipswich, but he only spent a few years there as his parents decided to move to London. At the age of eighteen he joined the Royal Navy where he spent three and a half happy years (his words) travelling around the world. Roy started courting with a Kettering girl and he eventually married her and came to live in Kettering. He got a job as a bus driver with United Counties; he also ran a stall on the market on Saturday mornings, selling jewellery. He eventually left his job as a bus driver to open a jewellery shop across the road from the Post Office. It was not long before he was looking for something else, and he decided to open a betting shop in Stamford Road, which proved to be very successful and led to him opening more shops in the area.

Roy Christie was an accomplished cricketer and he used to turn out regularly for Kettering Sunday XI. He enjoyed the comradeship, but most of all he enjoyed the social side. I asked him why he had been so generous to the league over the years and he replied " When I saw all the hard work that Reg Abbott and John Hill put into the running of the league I felt it was the least that I could do". Without Roys generosity it would have been very difficult for the league to carry on, and I think that it is highly probable that it would not have lasted as long as it did.

Jim Chaplin

There are some people who hate cricket, there are some people who like cricket and there are some people who just love it, and Jim Chaplin fell into the last category. I can remember back in the 1960s when the league programme had finished, Jim used to try and get a team together to play a few friendly matches.

Sometimes he would get carried away and arrange fixtures in October. In fact, on one occasion I had to tell him that we could not play on a particular Saturday as the clocks had gone back the previous week, (for the end of British Summer Time), and that it would be dark at four p.m.

Jim served the league for more than twenty years, ten of which he spent as secretary. In this office he carried out his duties extremely efficiently and he brought to the position a thoroughness which other incumbents could only hope to emulate. He also spent ten years on the executive committee where his experience and level headedness were invaluable assets. Jim played many years for Fuller, and when they changed their name to Ivanhoe he carried on for a few more years. Jim will be best remembered for his setting up of a new team in 1962 –Venturers (who set a qualifying age limit of a minimum of thirty-five years). So successful was this team that they carried on playing for a further thirty-two years, and they only stopped playing when the League was disbanded. Sadly, Jim is no longer with us, but if they play cricket up there it is a safe bet that he will be arranging a few friendlies.

Reg Abbott

Reg Abbott was elected as Chairman of the league in 1963, and he held the post until his resignation in 1986. Reg took his role of chairman very seriously and he always conducted management meetings in an orderly and methodical manner. When he was in the chair should anyone not be paying attention or should they transgress, it would only take a look from Reg to make them see the error of their ways. Reg put in a lot of hard work for the league, especially in the Six-a-Side tournament at the North Park, where more often than not he would be seen with a megaphone clasped in his hand keeping the spectators and players up to-date with the state of play.

Reg was captain of the successful Old Centralians side for a good many years and he had the ability to get the best out of his players. He was a highly respected captain, not only by his own team but by his opponents as well. He was a more than useful fast bowler and quite capable of rattling up a few runs. Reg is now a bowls player of some renown in the County, he is a popular player and he brings to that sport the same dedication that he brought to his cricket.

John Hill

John Hill once said to me that to run a cricket club you needed to be a contortionist, and it also helped if you were a bit of an idiot as well. When I asked him what he meant he said; "Well, we usually picked the team on a Tuesday and then I spent the rest of the week taking messages from people who could not play, which meant that I then had to run around like an idiot and get some one who could play. If I was lucky, by Saturday lunch time I would have a team of sorts." John would take the team kit balanced on the cross bar and the handle bars of his bicycle and attempt to ride from his home in Bryant Road to the North Park in Bath Road where his team, Holyoake, played their home matches, a distance of some two to three miles. It was not exactly a journey of a lifetime, but he usually managed to zig zag his way there.

John was secretary/treasurer of the Town League from 1968 until he resigned in 1986, and he was the longest serving secretary in it's history. During his term of office, John was only too willing to help any member of the County team during their benefit year and arrange matches for them at the North Park. These matches were always well attended and helped to swell the beneficiaries' coffers. John would also work very hard in organizing the Six-a-Side tournament every year, deciding how many grounds to use, allocating matches to pitches, making sure that the teams stared on time and generally seeing to it that the tournament ran as smoothly as possible. In 1973 the league decided to open its boundaries and to admit Wellingborough Indians to the league.   Previously the league was restricted to teams within the borough of Kettering and, in John's opinion; this move was the leagues salvation as there was a sudden influx, over the next few years, of Indian teams from Wellingborough wishing to join the league. All of this meant John's workload became somewhat heavier, but he welcomed this as it gave the league a new impetus and sustained them for a few more years.

John Hill is a born organizer and I have no doubt that while he was secretary of the league he loved every minute of it. Even when confronted at home by some irate team, to protest about some decision or some ruling that had not gone in their favour, he would just explain the rules to them with a smile on his face. He is passionate about his cricket and he played for Holyoake (or Havelock Works as it was) for more than forty years. Since retiring he has become a life member of the County Cricket Club and he spends his summers with his wife Norma, at the County ground idly watching the cricket. In the winter months John plays indoor bowls for the Kettering Lodge Bowling Club and he has become quite an accomplished player. He has also taken on the job of fixture secretary for them - of course!

Paul Rowney
Paul took over from John Hill in 1986 and he remained in that position until the league was disbanded in 1993. His task, from the outset, was not an easy one as the number of teams wishing to enter the League was getting fewer and fewer. During his term of office, approaches were made to the District League concerning amalgamation, but they did not seem interested in taking

this course of action. I think there were two reasons for this; firstly they were coming up to their centenary which was obviously important to them and secondly they did not relish the idea of playing on council grounds, especially with more than one game going on at the same time. Undeterred by this, Paul did all that was humanly possible to keep the League together, and a lot of credit is due to him for the efforts that he made.

Paul was a good all-round cricketer, and he was also a very loyal one. He played for the Post Office for twenty-one years, and he only stopped playing for them after they dropped out of the league. After a season with Nomads, who also dropped out of the league, he joined Tudors and he stayed with them until he retired from cricket all together. At the age of eighteen, he won the second division bowling averages taking 34 wickets at an average of 4.91. Paul could not attend the presentation dinner as he had been called up to do his national service. When Paul came home on his first leave from the army there was a postal order (for winning the bowling averages) waiting for him. He cashed it and bought himself some army socks to replace the ones that had been stolen from him.

When the old pavilion at the North Park was burned down and a new one was erected, Paul lobbied for some time for the pavilion to be dedicated to Albert Smith who was a well loved and respected man in Town League cricket. Thanks to Paul's efforts, on the 10th of September 1992 a commemorative plaque bearing Albert's name was unveiled.

They also served
Mr. A. Kilsby became the first secretary of the league in 1912, and the first Chairman was Mr. W. H. Brockhorst. They continued to hold office until 1915 by which time the First World War had broken out and cricket would have to take a back seat until 1920. From 1920 onward the league would have a further nine secretaries: Mr. T. A. Banks 1920-1929, Mr. C. C. Rainbow 1930-1939, Mr. C. Swales 1946-1949, Mr. H. Sharp 1950-1956, Mr. J. Chaplin, 1957-1962, 1964-1965, Mr. D. F. Clarke 1963, Mr. D. J. Short 1966-1967, Mr. J. Hill 1968-1985 and Mr. P. Rowney 1986-1993. There would also be a further five persons chairing the meetings: Mr. R. Sharp 1920-1939, Mr. R. Banks 1946-1954, Mr. D. F. Clarke 1955-1962, Mr. R. Abbott 1963-1985 and Mr. E. Dawkins 1986-1993. From 1950 onward, the secretary also took on the responsibility of treasurer, which had previously been a separate role, and it is worth mentioning that Mr. F. Smith undertook this task for over twenty years. A debt of gratitude is owed to the Leagues auditors such as Mr. A. Johnson, Mr. J. Short and Mr. M. J. Ward who always gave their services free of charge.

It would be remiss of me not to mention the sterling work that was done by the Executive Committee. I could not mention them all by name, as there are far too many who have served over the years. However, I should like to mention four men who between them gave over sixty year's service to the League; they are Ernie Sismey, Don Wright, Jack Taylor and Carl Howard. I know they worked very hard to improve the League as did many others.

All the people listed above helped to make it possible for the cricketers of the Town League to go out on a Saturday afternoon and enjoy themselves in the full knowledge that the League was in safe and sure hands.

Albert Smith

Even now, when I have occasion to walk from Montague Street to Stamford Road, when I get to Catesbury Street I still look for Albert's red bubble car. It is the only one that I ever saw; I never knew anyone else who owned one. John Sellars recalls the times when he was playing for Keystone; sometimes Albert would go to a match in the bubble car, and when he arrived at the ground it was not unusual to see six or seven players clamber out of the bubble looking somewhat dishevelled.

Albert Smith was born in 1912, which was the year that the Town League was formed. Albert first played in the league in 1931, for the Working Men's Club second team, and he picked up a winner's medal in his first season. He did not actually set the league alight although he did record figures of 6-14 against Leader Sports. He played for the Works for one more season and then, rather surprisingly, they resigned from the League. Miss Butchers Bible Class quickly moved in for him - it was a shrewd move on both their parts as they were to win the league in 1936/7/8 and Albert did more than his fair share towards their success. In 1936, Albert and B. Skinner took 93 wickets at an average of seven runs per wicket. Albert also finished the season with a batting average of seventeen. The following season, he represented the Town League against Wellingborough Works League and scored 38 runs out of the Kettering total of 59. He then went on to claim 4-26 despite Wellingborough scoring 108. In 1938, which was Miss Butchers last championship success, he teamed up with L. Cullip to take 106 wickets at a cost of six and a half runs. Albert took 54 of them, to comfortably win the Town League bowling averages.   There was to be only one more season before the Second World War broke out and, sadly, Miss Butchers Bible Class did not play in the Town League again.

After the war, Albert played for Nomads who only played friendly matches. However they did enter the Knock Out Cup, and they battled their way to the final. Their opponents were the Electricians whom they beat by five wickets, with Albert bowling three of them out for twenty-seven runs. For the next eight years he played for LMS and it was with this team that he played some of his best cricket. In 1949 they finished level on points with the Electricians only to lose the resulting play off game. The Railmens most successful season, however, was in 1952 when they won the second division section B title and the Kettering Association Knock Out Cup. That season Albert was top of the leagues second division batting and bowling averages. He scored 283 runs at an average of 40.40, and he won the bowling averages taking 45 wickets at 4.08. In one match against Tite and Garfirths he scored 59 not out in an undefeated opening partnership with Harry Marlow of 142. Then when Tites batted he took 6-15. In 1955 Albert joined Athletic and helped them to the First Division championship, and the following year (as the Crusaders) they won the Knock Out Cup. He continued to play for Crusaders until 1960 and then he joined for Casuals for one season.

In 1962 Albert was asked if he would be interested in coaching a cricket team from Keystone Boys Club, a local youth club whose headquarters were in Rockingham Road. Albert did not need to be asked twice and he jumped at the opportunity. They were all young boys up to the age of sixteen and would probably take some handling. This did not phase Albert, he was firm without being too authoritarian and he encouraged the boys to enjoy themselves, which they did. They were a joy to watch when they were fielding; they showed such enthusiasm, which is not always evident in young boys, and they were rewarded for their endeavours when they won the F. R. Brown Trophy for fielding in 1963. During his five-year spell with Keystone, Albert guided the team to the third division championship in 1963 and the Six-a-Side Cup in1966. A remarkable success rate in such a short time, and it really speaks volumes for Albert's qualities of leadership and his ability to get the best out of the boys. Whilst playing for Keystone he notched the first and only century of his career when he scored 100 not out against Barton B. That was in 1963 at the age of 51 years. In 1967 the new generation of boys were coming through and the older boys had to give way to make room for them. Consequently, the highly successful team was broken up, but they eventually formed their own club, which was one of the most successful teams in the Town League - the Taverners. Albert also decided to leave the club, and at the age of 55 he joined the Venturers (which was rather going to the other extreme). However, he enjoyed his cricket with them so much that he stayed with them until 1972 when he was in his sixtieth year.

Never one to resist a challenge, Albert took on the job of running another youth team, Christie Colts, who were sponsored by the Chairman of the Town League, Roy Christie. Albert spent six years with the Colts before he finally hung up his boots at the ripe old age of 67 years. He did not finish with cricket however and he went on to spend many years umpiring in the Town League.

The preceding paragraphs only give you a brief insight into Albert's career, it does not tell you what an exceptional cricketer he was; it does not tell you that he could bowl fast medium deliveries that zipped off the wicket, nor does it tell you that he could bowl off breaks and turn the ball two feet and that he was fleet of foot in the field and a very good batsman as well. All this he achieved in forty-six years of Town League cricket.

However, there was much more than this to the man, he was an honourable man, he was an honest man, he was a generous man in defeat and he was modest in victory, he never lost his temper nor did he fall out with anyone on a cricket field. Cricket was good to Albert Smith and he derived a great deal of pleasure from it. Yet he put much more back into the game than he ever took out of it, he was not only a role model to the youngsters of Keystone and Christie Colts, but he led by example and set a standard that all of us could only hope to emulate. Albert Smith sadly died on the 2nd June 1992 in his eightieth year and his death prompted many people to write to the Evening Telegraph to record their personal memories of him. The tribute from Roy Christie was the most appropriate when he described him as a true gentleman of sport.

A new pavilion had to be built at the North Park to replace the old one which, unfortunately, had been badly damaged by fire. The Council agreed, after many requests, that the pavilion would be dedicated to the memory of Albert, in recognition of his services to local cricket. So on the tenth of September 1992, Mrs. Ivy Steventon (Albert's sister) and Mr. Phil Sawford (council leader) unveiled the plaque which dedicated the pavilion to Albert.

Kettering Umpires Association
The association was formed in 1950. The list of umpires was made up of ex-cricketers with just one or two exceptions. For many years, teams had supplied their own umpires. This was fine until the occasion arose when the umpire needed to make a crucial decision and felt himself to be under too much pressure. Forming the association was an instant success. So popular was it that at one time there were over thirty umpires on the list, and they were able to supply two umpires for every town league game. They could not be accused of showing any bias now. They would make mistakes but they would be deemed to be honest ones.

Town League players could count themselves fortunate to have the luxury of neutral umpires, I am not aware of any other local league in a similar position. Derek Clarke left the Town League to take over the position of secretary for the Association and he held this post for a good many years, and a very fine job he made of it too, as did Bill Warren when he took over from Derek. The list of umpires contained the names of some of the finest players ever to play in the League; Albert Cartwright, Reg Green, Fred Smith, Roly Drew, Bunny Underwood and Norman Goodfellow to name just a few. It just goes to prove that the strength of the league was such that the very players who had graced the league with such distinction for so many years were now prepared to give up their time and to put something back into the game that had given them so much pleasure. Sadly in 1973, the Association had to be disbanded because of the decline in the number of members.

Chapter XII

Cup Competitions

The hoofs are on the road, boys,
They sing a merry catch:
O the suns at noon, and the years at June,
And we're driving to the match!

E. V. Lucas

Six-a-Side

In 1955 discussions took place between the League and the Kettering
Carnival Committee for the Blind in an attempt to find ways of raising
money for people with impaired sight or for those people who were totally
blind. After much discussion, the League came up with the idea of running a
Six-a-Side Competition, which would be played to a finish on the same day
(weather permitting of course). Mr. Edgar Towell kindly donated a trophy,
which would be known as the Edgar Towell Challenge Trophy. The venue
for the tournament would be the North Park ground in Bath Road, and in
1955 the first competition was staged.

The rules of the competition were quite simple; each team would
consist of a maximum of six players, each team would bat for a duration of
five overs and bowlers would be restricted to bowling one over only. Should
the bowler be called by the umpire for bowling a wide ball then the batting
side would be awarded four runs and an extra ball would be bowled. A team
was all out once it had lost five wickets, and the team scoring the highest
number of runs would be declared the winners - otherwise the normal rules
of cricket applied. The tournament was run on a knock out basis until there
were just two teams left to contest the final.

This venture was a truly remarkable one for local cricket, not only
for Town League sides. As the competition grew in popularity, teams from
all around the Kettering area were applying to enter. Some teams did not
have any affiliation to any cricket club they just wanted to join in the fun, if
in the process, they could help to raise money for charity, so much the better.
Sometimes as many as thirty six teams would enter, which necessitated two
grounds having to be used in the morning play, but usually the numbers were
kept down to thirty two. Play would commence in the morning at 10-30 and
the final would take place at approximately 7-30 in the evening, depending
on how kind the weather had been during the day. It was not unusual for the
final to finish at around 9pm.

The competition was usually held on the last Sunday in June and to most local cricketers it was the most eagerly awaited day of the season. It was an absolute carnival of cricket, full of excitement and anticipation. Not just for the cricketers, but for their families and also for those people who had no connections with any of the teams, who just came to watch and enjoy the day. Inevitably, they got caught up in the whole euphoria of the cricketing mayhem, because mayhem it sometimes was. Quite often there would be four matches going on at the same time and cricket balls would be flying all over the place. Not only did players have to keep their eyes on the game in which they were playing, but on all the other games. Bowlers who, under normal circumstances, could expect to be treated with due respect by batsmen, were quite often being dispatched contemptuously to all parts of the field. Batsmen could also be made to feel a little foolish, especially when falling to someone bowling, what could only be described as, donkey drops. But one aspect of the game that can only be described as amazing was the fielding. Players seemed to take on a new lease of life; some were seen to be plucking the ball out of the air one-handed, others were running thirty or forty yards to hold on to catches, and the ground fielding was sometimes brilliant. With so few fielders having to cover such a large area players were attaining speeds over the ground that they never thought themselves capable of.

Why then was it so popular? Other six-aside tournaments were run in other towns within the county. Why was this one always the most sought after to enter and indeed to win? Was it possibly that the attraction for players and spectators alike was the fact that there were four games going on at the same time, and there was always some thing to see. Or maybe the North Park was a wonderful ground for a competition such as this. I remember Keith Andrew the Northants and England wicket keeper reporting on the match for the Evening Telegraph, writing, "I was amazed at what I saw, impossible catches being held, balls were flying every where, and I saw hitting like I had never seen before." He concluded by saying that the entertainment provided was a credit to the Town League and to all the players that had taken part.

The Six-a-Side endured for nearly fifty years, and in all that time it never lost its attraction to the players or to the many hundreds of spectators who would not leave until the last ball had been bowled. It was a truly magical day, a very entertaining day and a day that gave so much pleasure to so many people, and it also raised many thousands of pounds for a very worthy cause.

Kettering Association Knock Out Cup

You always knew when there was a Knock Out match at the North Park because around about 6-30pm Uncle Fred, who lived in Eskdale Street with Aunt Jess, would clip his bike clips on and give Aunt Jess a peck on the cheek as he informed her that he was off to the allotment to get some vegetables for the next day. He would then pedal to the North Park, prop his bike against the wall, which ran the full length of the ground, and watch the game without ever going inside the ground. In between innings he would climb aboard his trusty steed and pedal furiously to his allotment (which was situated off the Weekly Road at the Warkton Turn), pick some vegetables and return poste haste to watch the rest of the match. Whether Aunt Jess knew about Uncle Fred's little deception, I don't know, but if she did she never let on.

The Kettering Association Knock Out Cup began in 1929, and the semi-finals and the final were usually played at the North Park. The Men's Own Institute won it the first year and again the second year. After their second success the Men's Own were presented with the winners Trophy by Mr. Harry Potter, the well known Kettering Councilor, and he astounded every one by remarking that more teams should enter the competition and not to be afraid of the Men's Own, who were a very good side. Mr. Potter's words must have touched a raw nerve because from that time on the tournament attracted a large number of entries for many years to come.

Every Town League side entered the tournament and there were also many other sides such as Town CC, W. B.Wrights, Old Cytringanians, Teachers, Southgate, Isham, Oakley, and many others. But if one team had to be singled out who did more than any other to raise the profile of the Knock Out Cup, then it must surely be Frank Wrights. The Wright family was certainly the most famous cricketing family in the county. They played an annual match with Kettering CC, and on one occasion they had to play fifteen aside so that no one in the family would be disappointed. They provided players for the county side and the Club and Ground. In 1932 they reached the final of the Knock Out Cup (scoring a massive 139 against a Kettering Evening XI), and went on to win the match by 45 runs. The following year they again reached the final. This time they scored 136 runs to beat Freeman Hardy and Willis who themselves scored 128. They made it three finals in a row in 1934, and a hat trick of wins, when they beat William Timpsons by 114 runs to 95. People had never seen entertainment like it, and it was estimated that something like 9,000 spectators turned out to watch the three finals. The scores that were achieved in those three games were never surpassed, and Frank Wrights had set a benchmark that other teams could only dream of attaining.

In 1935, Frank Wrights found it necessary to resign from the competition; this was after the executive committee had ordered their semi-final match with Timpsons to be replayed, which they refused to do. Apparently Wrights were unable to raise a team for the semi-final and sought permission from the executive committee of the Association to play an unregistered player. The executive committee gave their blessing providing that neither of the two players put forward by Wrights was used. One of the named players did play in the semi-final match, which Wrights duly won. An executive meeting was held on the Monday and the committee ordered the game to be replayed which infuriated the captain of Wrights, Mr. Bert Wright, who stated that he was not having the Association picking his team for him, and after consulting with his players they decided not to replay the match. The dispute caused quite a stir and dozens of letters were sent to the Evening Telegraph regarding the matter. Some were on the Associations side and some spoke up for Wrights. But the upshot was that Wrights never appeared in the competition again, which was a great pity as they had done so much to popularize the competition.

In 1936 it was Kettering CC's turn to lift the trophy and so keen were they to do well that they included the likes of H.J.H. Lamb, K.R.Greasley and Edgar Towell in their team to play Crusaders. They won the match in style by nearly one hundred runs; Lamb and Greasley scoring 53 and 40 respectively and Edgar Towell 7-10, including a hat-trick, in the Crusaders score of 26. Kettering also helped to make the competition such a great success. All told they won the cup over twenty times and the nearest any other team came to this remarkable feat was the Men's Own. The Men's Own won the cup on six occasions and three of their successes came during the war when only a handful of teams entered. When the Town were in the final of the Knock Out Cup, the crowd were always routing for the other team. It did not matter who they were, they could be the most disliked team in the Town League but, when they played the Town, everybody was behind them, willing them to win. The Town took it all in good part however and usually they came out on top, it was extremely difficult to get the better of them in a final. You stood a much better chance if you played them in one of the early rounds at the Glebe farm say, where the wickets were unpredictable and tended to fly a bit, unlike the flat track they were used to on the Town ground.

One man who did more for the competition than anyone else was Harry Coe. Harry was secretary for an incredible forty-three years and even after his resignation due to ill health, he still continued to serve on the committee of the Association for some years to come. On his retirement, Harry was presented with a silver salver and a transistor radio by the president of the Association, Mr. A.J.H. Lamb. The presentation was held at the Kettering Town pavilion on 9th May 1975.

Harry played for St. Mary's Bible Class before the war and was something of an allrounder. However, it was in his capacity as secretary to the Kettering Cricket Association that he is best remembered. Not only did he organize the Knock Out Cup but he went around all the grounds with his collecting box ensuring that as much money as possible was raised for charity, a truly remarkable man!

There were many exciting finals and to give readers a taste of some of these I have selected what I consider to be three of the best.

Freeman Hardy and Willis v Frank Wrights 1932

Freeman Hardy and Willis batted first and Maurice Dunkley and J. Richardson put together a useful opening partnership of 30 runs, before W. King bowled Richardson for 13. D. Parker then came in, and with his score on 5 he was forced to retire when he was struck a painful blow on the hand. King then bowled Hope and Chapman in successive balls. Maurice Dunkley was undeterred by this however, and he went on to a magnificent undefeated score of 70, which included 10 fours. S. Roughton (17) and R. Hales (11) ably supported him and they eventually posted a score of 128-5 in their allotted time of one hour and ten minutes. In reply, Frank Wrights started well with A. Smith scoring 33 in quick time, it was just the start that Frank Wrights needed. B. Wright then came in and hit a quick 9 runs, but the game changed dramatically when S. Wright was out for 44, brilliantly caught by Dunkley. After this, the play became very intense with the result in doubt until Nick Wright took charge, and with some lusty blows finally settled the match with some six minutes to spare. This final produced the highest number of runs ever scored in the final of the Knock Out Cup. However, some people are never satisfied, and a spectator was prompted to write to the Evening Telegraph complaining of the time wasting tactics employed by one of the teams. This seems a little strange when you consider that 264 runs were scored in two hours and twenty minutes.

Scores:

Freeman Hardy and Willis		Frank Wrights	
M. Dunkley not out	70	A.Smith c Richardson b Roughton	33
J. Richardson b King	13	S. Wright c Dunkley b Sharman	44
D. Parker retired hurt	5	B. Wright c Parker b Roughton	9
H. Hope b King	0	W.King not out	11
H. Chapman b King	0	N. Wright b Richardson	25
S.Roughton c King b N.Wright	17	Extras	14
R. Hales b King	11	Total (total for 4 wickets)	136
A. C. Clements not out	8		
Extras	4		
Total (for 5 wickets) 128		Frank Wrights beat Freeman Hardy and Willis	

Working Men's Club v Kettering July 1967

Working Men's won the toss and elected to bat first. Fred Beasley and
Barry Essam opened the batting and they went off like the proverbial train;
they ran for everything. If it went through to the wicket keeper they ran, if
they hit it they ran, if it hit their pads they ran, they really put the Town
fielders under so much pressure that a lot of mistakes began to creep into
their fielding. Altogether they put on 49 runs in less than 6 overs, with
Beasley scoring 16 and Essam 20. This gave the innings the perfect
foundation and allowed Barry Foster (12) and John Lawman (12) and some
of the others to bat soundly and take the total to 115-6 off the allotted 18
overs. Kettering made a confident start to their innings and at the half way
mark they had made 59-2 for the loss of Brian Sanders and John Marriott.
At this stage they were well in contention and they were still going well
when John Popham was out with the score at 69-3. But then the whole
complexion of the game changed in the course of one over. Peter Larcombe
and Mick Reed were dismissed in consecutive balls by Alan Coles, and then
A. Connolly was brilliantly caught by Alan Stapleton off the last ball of the
over. At 72-6 the Town were really struggling but they managed to hang in
there and when the last over arrived they needed 14 runs to win with two
wickets remaining. The first ball of the over was called a no ball and the
second one was a wide. The next five balls yielded seven runs and so the
last ball arrived with the Town needing four runs to tie the match. But
luckily for the Works the batsmen missed the ball and it went straight
through to wicket keeper, Ray Poulson, and a truly exciting match ended in
victory for the Works by four runs.

 N.B. I was responsible for bowling that last over and after the first two
balls I would have gladly changed places with anyone on that ground, it was
one of the most nerve wracking experiences of my life.

Crusaders v Kettering July 1969

Derek Plews and Mick Ward opened the batting for Crusaders and they
batted steadily if not spectacularly. Apart from Mick Ward, who scored 19
runs, none of the Crusaders batsmen were able to get going and they
slumped to 60-6. There were only two overs remaining. Barry Maples
came in at the fall of the second wicket and had only managed to score 10
runs, all of which had come in singles. He then proceeded to score 23 of the
25 runs added in those last 2 overs to take the score to a respectable 86-7.
Kettering quickly found themselves in trouble when they batted. A brilliant
caught and bowled by Geoff Toseland to get rid of the dangerous Briance
and the early dismissals of Popham and Sanders had them reeling on 21-3.
Keith Arthey steadied the ship a little with 24 and then Keith Williams struck

the luckless Ollie Dalziel for two fours and two sixes to bring the game round into Ketterings favour. It came down to the last over (bowled by Roy Christie), and what an over it was! Needing six runs to win, Town scored nothing off the first ball, they scampered a single off the second, the third ball yielded another single, the fourth ball was a dot ball, the fifth was a dot ball, which meant that they now needed a four off the last ball to win the match. Every fielder was dispatched to the outfield, the boundary seemed fully protected, surely the Town could not win the game now? Spaces between the fielders were at an absolute minimum. The Kettering batsman struck the ball with all his might, there was a loud crack as the ball flew off the middle of the bat, and lo and behold, the ball, somehow squeezed in between the fielders and over the line for a boundary. The Town had won a most famous victory.

Scores

Crusaders		Kettering	
Plews b Sanders	6	Popham c Toseland b Lenton	11
Ward st Horrell b Heygate	19	Briance c & b Toseland	2
Pridmore b Freestone	0	Sanders c Lenton b Toseland	2
Maples not out	33	Arthey c Plews b Christie	24
Toseland c Sanders b Heygate	5	Freestone c Ward b Pell	5
Pell b Turner	0	Williams b Pell	29
Dalziel st Horrell b Heygate	2	Horrell not out	5
Christie c Arthey b Williams	9	Hindle lbw Christie	0
Lenton not out	2	Coles b Maples	0
Extras	10	Heygate not out	6
Total (for 7 wickets)	86	Extras	3
		Total (for eight wickets)	87

Kettering beat Crusaders by 1 run

The Knock Out Cup competition lasted for 57 years and the people of Kettering took the competition to their hearts. They would flock to the North Park in their hundreds to watch the final, and it was a date everyone pencilled in on their calendar. To the cricketers of the Town, it was something that you looked forward to, the disappointments, the heartbreaks and the occasional triumphs. It could also be very intimidating, playing in the final in front of a large crowd. There were plenty of butterflies around on that day. There is just one note of sadness; in 1985 it was decided at the Annual General meeting of the Association that entries would be by invitation only and that those invites would not extend to any Town League sides. This was a monumental error to exclude the very teams that had been instrumental in making the competition such a success over the years. Not surprisingly, 1985 was the last year of the Kettering Association Knock Out Cup competition.

Chapter XIII

More Players and Grounds

The shadows fall, the day is done,
The battle over and the victory won
Francis Colgate Benson.

Unlike first class cricket, local cricket deeds and events are not recorded for posterity; indeed why should they be? Who cares what happened to two factory teams playing a game of cricket sixty years ago or twenty years ago. Well a lot of the players cared, some of those players played the game for twenty, thirty or even forty years, you do not get that sort of dedication if you do not care about the game. There are those who would say that our cricket is not real cricket, well we did not play on wickets that were as true as a billiard table, nor were we good enough to earn a living at the game, but we played for the sheer enjoyment that we derived from playing, and it gave us the opportunity to pit ourselves against other teams in friendly battle. So what I would like to do in this chapter is to first look at some of the players who played in the league in the early days, and then I would like to bring you some of the cricketers who played in the 1930s, the 1940s,and later into the 1980s and early 1990s. Unfortunately, there is not anyone alive today who could tell us about the players who played in the league before the First World War or, about those that played in the league in the early 1920s, so I would like to recall just a few who played in this period and to recollect on some of their exploits. I would also like to take you on stroll around the grounds that were used.

In the very first year of the Town League, 1912, two pairs of fast bowlers made their mark. The first pair who played for Men's Own were H. Towell and H. Smith who between them took 93 wickets at an average of 4.00, and they were considered to be quite a handful. The Working Men's Club also had a lively opening attack in R. Sharp and G. Coe and they accumulated 119 wickets between them at an average 5.19,and although these figures were obtained in all matches they were still a force to be reckoned with. Tom Freeman and G. Freestone were another pair of bowlers who were quite successful and they took a number of wickets, although they were not considered nearly as formidable as the Men's Own and Works pairs, they did a very good job for Co-op Clothiers.

F. Bull of Mobbs and Lewis was an allrounder of immense talent and he was both a prolific run maker and wicket taker and he very nearly became the first player in the league to take all ten wickets in a match, when he took 9-9 against Church Institute in 1913. Another prominent allrounder was R. Masters of the Men's Own who turned in many good performances with both bat and ball.

In this period leading up to the First world War there are not many reports that give us an insight as to who were the batsmen of the day. The only exception to this was F. Wilson of Miss Butchers who, it would seem, was an outstanding batsman. Before we leave pre-war time I should like to mention a report, which appeared in the Evening Telegraph thus, "Mr. E. Mutton in his first season with St Mary's took thirteen wickets, more than any other bowler in the league, and he is to be commended on this feat. However, his batting was woefully below standard."

Cricket resumed after the war in 1920, and many cricketers made their presence felt in the first half of the decade. F. Ellis and J. Piddington of the Athletic Club were both very good batsmen scoring runs consistently. Barton Wanderers also had two players who scored a lot of runs in A. Spence and C. Seddon. Probably the best batsman of this period was A. Biddlecombe of North Park who made many significant scores for them. He was aided and abetted by P. Jeffecoat who himself was a heavy scorer. Not to be outdone, the Men's Own had their own wielders of the willow in A. Pickford and F. Jeffrey. H. Liquorish of Men's Own, I. Tomalin of Co-op Clothiers and B. Course of Gravestocks were the most successful of the allrounders and in the bowling stakes the most honours went to A. Bailey of North Park, T. Freeman of Men's Own. H. Chapman of St. Andrews and H. Wilson of Barton Wanderers.

Moving from the late 1920s and into the 1930s we find that more and more players were now coming to the fore and the standard of cricket was improving as the league was able to attract more cricketers. B. Skinner (Miss Butchers), C. Sherbourne (Freeman Hardy and Willis) W. Woolmer and P. Curchin (both of Freeman Hardy and Willis), H. Townsend (St Marys) L. Cullip (Thomas Birds) A. Hunt (Wilson and Watsons) H. Sculthorpe (Kaycee) L. Weatherall (Barton Wanderers) and O. Pearson (North Park) were some of the top bowlers of this period. But, the most fearsome bowling attack was that of Len Shipley and George (Chokey) Meadows who opened the bowling for Thomas Birds. They were fast and accurate and they could be very intimidating, they quite often bowled unchanged throughout an innings and many teams found them very difficult to cope with. I spoke to Reg Green and Dennis Hefford who both played against them and they both agreed that they were the best pair of fast bowlers that they ever faced in the Town League. Reg and Dennis are both in their 84th year and played Town League cricket in the 1930s and well into the 1950s. They were both allrounders of quality and they both spoke highly of each other.

There is one other bowler who, in the words of Reg Green, was a little bit special and certainly too good for the Town League - Bill Dunham. He bowled slow left arm spinners and he was able to mesmerize most of the batsmen he bowled to. Apart from taking all ten wickets at a cost of 48 runs for Mobbs and Lewis against Wilson and Watsons in 1935, he also turned in many other match winning performances. Bill Dunham was also an accomplished batsman as was seen in 1938 when he finished the season as runner up in the Leagues batting averages, scoring 305 runs at an average of 21:78. Incidentally, he also finished as runner up in the bowling averages with 60 wickets at an average of 6:56 in the same year.

I do not think that anyone would argue with the choice of the Town Leagues finest batsman. The first player to score a century in the League, who batted with great flair and imagination and who was certainly no respecter of bowling. He was, of course, Maurice Dunkley of Freeman Hardy and Willis. Maurice was the only Town League player to play for the County, he played for them in the late 1930s and when war broke out he promised to play for them after the war, but for whatever reason he never went back. Reg Green, who worked and played cricket with him, speaks of him as being a modest man who continued to play in evening matches for Freeman Hardys whilst still playing for the County from 1937-1939. Dunkley played 6 innings for the County; scoring 904 runs at an average of 15.06, with a highest score of 70 not out made against Yorkshire. In that innings he dispatched the great Hedley Verity for no fewer than seven boundaries. Maurice also played football for Manchester City, the Cobblers and the Poppies.

There were some very fine batsmen in the league at this time and one of the most successful was Albert Cartwright. He made many big scores for Thomas Birds including a century against Kaycee. He also kept wicket and was considered to be one of the best wicket keeper/batsmen in the League. Dennis Hefford, when speaking of him, described him as a brilliant batsman, a good wicket keeper, a kindly man and a true sportsman.

Another batsman, who many thought was the equal of Albert, was an old and dear friend of mine; Fred Garley. Fred once told me that on match days he would make a point of having a lie down for an hour before the match so that he was physically and mentally fresh for the battle ahead. Some would say that that was beyond the call of duty but that was the kind of man Fred was, and it certainly paid off because he consistently made good scores. Fred, like Albert, continued to play after the war until the mid 1950s.

Trevor Coleman was another class act who made his runs with style and panache and he was the mainstay of the Mobbs and Lewis team. These were not the only three good batsmen of their day however, there were many more who turned in impressive performances; A. Goodall won the Town League batting averages in 1938 with an average of 24.00. L. Hales of Wilson and Watson had his best year in 1933 the year he scored a century against Havelock Works. G. Wallington of Gravestocks made a century in 1938 against Wilson and Watsons. L. Farrell Fuller was a big hitter and if it was his day he could amass a lot of runs quickly and Arthur Lawrence who played for Thomas Birds was another batsman who was capable of making big scores. One player who is worthy of mention is Dennis Parker, who captained Freeman Hardy and Willis in the late 1930s, indeed he captained the team to success in the 1937 Knock Out Cup when they beat Kettering Thursday in the final. Dennis used to act as the mobile librarian for Kettering and District, taking his vanload of books to people who had difficulty in getting to the library. But I think Dennis is best remembered for his singing and he was much better known as Dodi Parker.

Three allrounders stood apart from all the others at this time and the first of these was W. Julian who played for Stocks. In 1938 he had a tremendous season, he won the Leagues batting averages with an average of nearly 40 runs. He also won the bowling averages when he took 54 wickets at a cost of 4.07. In the same season he scored 101 runs against the Gas Company. C. Freestone of Miss Butchers BC was an influential player in Miss Butcher's dominance in the late thirties. He won the league batting averages in 1939 but his bowling was his strongest weapon and he was a cricketer to be respected. It is uncanny, how Havelock Works seem to have this knack of finding allrounders, and they certainly found one in Bert Russell. I have spoken to many people who played with, or against, Bert and I have yet to find one who did not think that he was the finest allrounder of his day. Indeed, many thought him to be the best allrounder that ever played in the League. He was a perfectionist and a real student of the game. John Hill who played with him after the war, told me that, after a particularly bad season by his standards, Bert decided to call it a day and retire from cricket altogether. If he could not perform to the standard that he had set himself then he would not play at all.

Due to the outbreak of the second World War in 1939, the League was forced to suspend operations until 1946 which was obviously a big disappointment to all the players, however a good many of them played again after the war and appeared to be as good as ever. There were many other players who I have not mentioned yet and who were certainly amongst the best players that ever played Town League cricket. Fred Smith who played for Fuller, bowled quick off -breaks and he was regarded by many as the finest spin bowler that the League ever produced. He certainly took a huge amount of wickets in his career. The County would quite often play a representative side chosen from the League and the County players would refer to Fred as the poor mans Jim Laker, which was praise indeed. Bill Chester who played for Rifles was a very good medium pace bowler and a fine batsman too. Roly Drew, considered by many to be the leagues best wicket-keeper, was also an accomplished batsman and a fierce hitter of the ball. Joe Bent, who sadly passed away recently, was a batsman of immense talent and he has two league centuries to his name. He was also a very good change bowler, and in 1971 when playing for Tite and Garfirths against Taverners II he had the distinction of scoring a century, and when Taveners batted he proceeded to take a hat-trick; a unique performance by anyone's standards.

We are now left with the late 70s through to 1993, which was sadly the end of the Town League, as the period after the war has been previously covered. This is a period in the Leagues history, which is difficult to define as more than half the centuries that were scored in the league were scored in this period of time. There is a danger when looking at the merits of cricketers and cricket teams of overstating or understating their abilities, and I think that you should judge them as they were at that time, and not make comparisons with players of a different era.

Steve Bailey who played for Harlequin was a dominant figure in the 80s. He set an all time record by scoring three league centuries. He was also one of the leagues most successful bowlers. Another fine batsman was Dave Fenwick who scored two centuries and came close to another one when he made 96 for Crusaders against East Carlton. Mark Wittering of Tudors also scored two centuries and he made the highest score of 150, which he holds jointly with Mark Hanby of Venturers. Other century makers during this period were: Mark Mason, (Ram Sports) Dean Pridmore, (Venturers) Steve Kendall, (Ram Sports) John Warwick, (Tudors) Prakash (Kangos) K. Patel, (Kangos) John Kemp, (Ram Sports) Gordon Livesy, (Crusaders) Peter Daniels, (Tudors) David Beale, (Holyoake) Neil Mobbs, (Melton) and Roger Fox (Bletsoe.) Other notable performers with the bat were Dilip Patel, (Jumbos) Mukesh, (Flamingos) Ian Starsmore, (Christie Colts) Chris Fulcher, (Old Cents and Crusaders) and Tim Osborn (Christie Colts.)

The league was rich in allrounders and I will name just a few who were prominent in the 1980s. Ricky Cooper is a name that comes readily to mind, he was a no nonsense batsman and he hit the ball extremely hard. He was also a very fine bowler, quite capable of bowling a side out. In 1980 he was voted the Player of the Year. Steve Walton was another player who was held in high regard. He was a stylish batsman and a more than useful medium pace bowler. He was voted the Young Player of the Year in 1979 and he was proving to be as good an allrounder as his father Pete was. Gordon Livesy, the ex-Poppies goalkeeper, was a very talented cricketer, and although he played in the League earlier for Keystone I have included him during his spell with Crusaders. He could, on his day, bowl very fast and he caused the batsman many problems. He was also a very useful batsman and he played many good innings for his team. He was elected as the Player of the Year in 1979.

Many Indian teams from the Wellingborough area participated in the league during this period and one of the best players to travel along the A509 to Kettering was Keiron Patel of Kangos. He turned in many fine batting performances which were underlined when he scored a century against Holyoake in 1990. He was also one of Kangos main bowlers. Kanshik and A. Joshi who both played for Wellingborough Indians could also be relied upon to perform well with both bat and ball.

Brian Bambridge, of Venturers, came into League cricket after many years of playing friendly cricket for Southgate and he quickly made the transition, proving himself to be an accomplished cricketer who liked to hit the ball hard. He was also an extremely useful spin bowler. Dave Gilbert played many a match winning innings for Crusaders and he was also a very capable bowler. Kelly Meagan who played for Christie Colts was beginning to show a great deal of promise with both bat and ball, and it came as no surprise when he was voted as the Young Player of the Year for 1981.

Successful bowlers during this period included Ken Brock (Melton), R. Thomas (Bletsoe), David Holmes (Crusaders - son of Terry, who for many years had been the scourge of Town League batsmen), Dale Steventon of Saracens whose father was also a very fine bowler. Mick Goodhall was another ex-Poppies player and he turned in many useful bowling performances for the Venturers. Dougie Bellamy who also played for the Venturers was a bowler who could be relied upon to regularly get amongst the wickets. Terry Flak was the mainstay of the Bletsoe attack and the same could be said of the Flamingos bowler Manher Patel

Around the Grounds:

The Grange
Situated on the Weekley Road, the Grange ground was first used for Town League matches in the 1920s by Working Men's Club, who played there until the mid 1930s. It was then taken over by Wilson and Watsons who transformed the ground into one of the finest grounds in the league. This was mainly due to the fact that they built a brand new pavilion on the site, and they were able to supply a groundsman to look after the pitch. The ground was on the right hand side of the road as you walk towards Weekley, the Grange shopping precinct now occupies that site.

Gas Street

John Stockburn used to graze cattle on a field at the bottom of Gas Street, and in 1900 when he heard that Kettering Cricket Club were looking for a ground to play their matches on he offered them the use of this field, providing that they did not interfere with the grazing of his cattle. Kettering accepted his offer, but they only took up the option for one season before they moved to another ground in the Headlands. Some years later, Men's Own Institute began playing Town League and District League matches on the ground and a small pavilion was built. This was quite a pretty ground, a wall used to run along the Gas Street side of the ground, its only drawback was that it tended to get waterlogged after heavy rain. The Men's Own continued to play their matches there until 1956. Gas Street has since been renamed Meadow Road. The ground was opposite the Kettering Gas Company, it is now a play area for children, and it is also used occasionally for car boot sales. Otherwise the ground remains much the same today as it was when Men's Own played there.

Gas House Field

Kettering Gas Company played their home matches at the Lower Street ground. The ground was at the bottom of Lower Street with the Slade Brook running along side and the railway bridge on the other side of the road. The Gas Company played there for a number of years and they used to attract good support from the Lower Street and Northall Street residents. Unlike the Gas Street ground they did not have the flooding problems to contend with. Lidls supermarket and the recently closed Esso Garage now occupy the site.

Water Mill

Sometimes this ground was referred to as the Water Mill or the Mill. John Hill recalls his father telling him of the time when as a very young boy he would go down to the ground to watch his father who played for the Working Men's Club. At teatime John's father would have to dash off, on foot, to the Evening Telegraph offices with the latest score to enable it to go into the stop press. Town League matches were played there in the 1920s. To reach the ground you needed to go along Windmill Lane, which is now Windmill Avenue. In between what are now Naseby Road and Deeble Road, was a lane, you went along the lane, through some allotment fields and finally you reached the ground. The ground was so called because there was a Windmill and a Mill House in Windmill Lane which have now long gone. A garage now stands on the site, near to Mill Road.

Recreation Ground

The recreation ground, or the Rec. as it was affectionately known, was associated with the Town League for at least 75 years, and it has played host to some of the Town Leagues finest sides namely Fuller/Ivanhoe, Old Centralians, British Legion, Miss Butchers BC and British Railways, to name just a few. In the 1955 season there were ten teams who were allocated pitches on the Rec., which meant that there were five matches being played at the same time. But, strangely enough, accidents were few and far between. The wickets, although they were all inclined to slope from leg to off or from off to leg depending upon the direction you were bowling from, were the truest wickets in the league. The ground always appeared to be on the soft side and perhaps it was the sub-soil, rather than the preparation, which made the wickets better

Church Institute Field.

Church Institute Field was used for Town League cricket from the outset until the 1920s. All the church teams played there including St. Andrews, St. Mary's, Miss Butchers, Church Institute and many more. It was extremely difficult to pinpoint the actual location of the ground, but with the help of Andrea Pettingale from the Kettering Public Library we decided that it was situated in the Queen St/Green Lane area of the town, somewhere behind the site now occupied by Beddows Car Sales premises.

Headlands

Town League cricket was first played at the Headlands in the 1930s and matches continued to be played there until 1959. It was not a pretty ground and the wickets left a lot to be desired. The outfield was bare in places, and as hard as concrete. It was covered in what was more like straw than grass and you took your life in your hands if you dared to get your body behind the ball when you were fielding. When cricket resumed after the war it continued to be played at the Headlands for a further thirteen years, and in all that time only four teams played there. I think they were grateful when Town League Cricket bade the Headlands a not so fond farewell.

Rockingham Road

Athletic Club was not the only team to play at Rockingham Road,as they shared the use of the ground with the Poppies. A matting wicket would be laid out in the centre of the football pitch, but how the boundaries were defined remains a mystery. Perhaps the perimeter markings of the football pitch were used or maybe boundary markers were laid out. Matches were played there in the 1920s, although Reg Abbott recollects the Old Centralians playing a match against the Athletic there in the 1940s.

108

Lewis Road

The Lewis Road ground, which is situated off Pytchley Road, was owned by the Kettering Industrial Co-operative Society. Cricket and football were played there in the 1930s and into the early 1950s. The cricket team played under the name KICS in the beginning, but this was later changed to Kaycee. However, in the 1950s the cricket club was informed that they would have to vacate the field and they transferred to Glebe Farm. They subsequently became known as Glebe. Part of the ground has been taken over by the Southfield School, the rest of the ground remains much the same today.

Glebe Farm

Glebe Farm is situated in Weekly Glebe Road, and is best remembered as a football ground, where matches in the Kettering Amateur League and other games took place. Facilities, as one would expect from a farm building, were very poor and the tin bath there was legendary. It was a communal bath which was filled up just before the final whistle blew, and those players who were unfortunate enough to be the last ones in the bath were probably putting more mud on their bodies than they were taking off. It started to be used for cricket as well as football after the Second World War, and Kettering Borough Council eventually had the old farm building demolished and a new pavilion was built which incorporated proper changing rooms, showers and a refreshment lounge. It was a vast field and it accommodated five pitches. If the weather was inclement it could be a cold and un-inviting place as the only pitch where you could seek shelter from torrential rain and gale force winds was the pavilion pitch. For the rest of the teams there was no sanctuary or shelter from the elements. But on a warm sunny day there was no better place to be. Cricket was played there until the 1980s and football is still played there today.

North Park

The Poppies played their home matches at the North Park in the late 1800s and they continued to play there until 1897 when they moved to their present ground in Rockingham Road. For the next few years cycling and athletics were a feature of the activities taking place at the North Park, but in 1912, the year that the Town League was formed, it was used solely for cricket. League matches would be played there for the duration of the leagues existence. It became synonymous with local cricket, for as well as League matches being played there, it would host the Knock Out Cup semi-finals and Final and the Six-a-Side Tournament and representative matches between the League and other leagues in the county. Matches were also arranged between a League XI and a Northamptonshire CCC XI. These matches usually took place when a player from the County was taking a benefit. On two nights a week practice nets were put up and there was always a good attendance on these nights. The practice wickets were concrete with a matting laid over the concrete, these proved to be somewhat dangerous and the council, who owned and maintained the ground, were finally persuaded to have grass practice wickets laid.

For those people who played local cricket one name is etched in the mind when they think of the North Park and that name is Cyril Beard. Cyril was the groundsman at the North Park for thirty years, but he was much more than a groundsman he was more like a curator. He would tend the ground with loving care and woe betides anyone who did not treat his ground with the utmost respect. There was a path running around the perimeter of the ground and if you so much as put one foot on the grass and that foot was not wearing a cricket boot you would be chastised unmercifully and told in no uncertain terms to get off the grass. It did not matter to Cyril whether you were man or boy if you transgressed then you would feel the sharp end of his tongue. For all this, Cyril was a much liked and respected man, after all he was protecting our interests and ensuring that the ground was in the best possible condition for us to play cricket on. On one occasion, according to his son Robert, he had to seek the assistance of the local bobby whilst having difficulty removing children who were trespassing on the hallowed turf. The policeman came to his aid, but unfortunately, he was on a bicycle and rode it over the centre wicket. Needless to say, Cyril thought twice about asking for future assistance!

Cricket is no longer played at the North Park; it is now used primarily for football by the town's youngsters. So it is nice to know that it is being put to good use, but what would Cyril make of it?

A group of future Town Leaguers at the Town ground being coached by former Northants opening batsman, Percy Davis (1950).

Venturers circa 1990
Back Row (l to r): D. Barrie, D. Rodwell, S. Goodhall,
M. Coles, M. Hanby, D. Pridmore
Front Row: A. Coles, C. Mobbs, M. Goodhall, D. Coles, L. Fisher
N.B.The age criteria had been somewhat reduced by this stage.

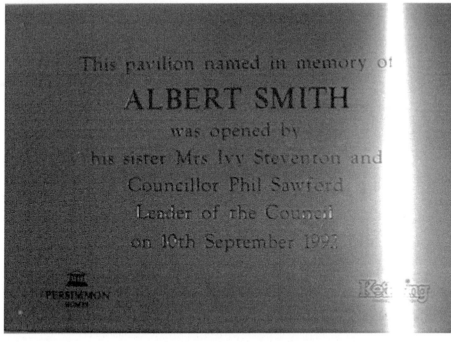

The plaque, adorning the new pavilion at the North Park, dedicated to the memory of Albert Smith.

The North Park (2005), once the Mecca of local cricket, now looks a forlorn sight. Oh that pavilion!

Northants and Pakistan allrounder Mushtaq Mohammad presents Fred Beasley with the Clubman of the Year award at the Working Mens annual dinner. Looking on are Ray Poulson (centre) and Stuart Moore (far left).

Taverners: one of the League's most successful sides in the Seventies.
Back Row (l to r): J. Ingram (Umpire), Not Known, M. Smith, S. Weston,
M. Ostle, J. Beale, A. Garley, scorer
Front Row: L.Weekes, L. Rowney, B. Foster, F. Beasley, T. Lewis

```
                                        J. S. Hill,
                                        Hon Sec.
                                        56 Bryant Road,
                                        Kettering.


    J. Sellars,                                   24/7/68
    13 St. Giles Close,
    Kettering.


    Dear Sir,

           I have the pleasure in notifying you of
    your selection for the Kettering Town Cricket
    League team, to play against the Kettering
    and District Cricket League team at the
    Kettering Town Cricket Ground, Northampton
    Road, on Sunday 25th. August, time 2.15.


                        Yours faithfully,



                        Mr. J. S. Hill.
                        Hon. Sec.
```

John Sellars receives his letter of selection for the Town League XI versus the
District League XI

Weekley and Warkton: winners of the Kettering Association Cup 1983.
Back Row (l to r): D. Clarke, P. Clarke, S. Weston, C. Issitt, T. Walklate, L Rowney.
Front Row: J. Sellars (sen..), M. Ostle, O. Dalziel, B. Foster, J Sellars (jun.).

Mr. Thomas Bird: League President 1946-1955

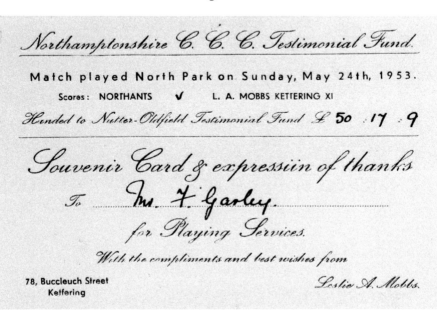

Northamptonshire C. C. C. Testimonial Fund.

Match played North Park on Sunday, May 24th, 1953.

Scores: NORTHANTS ✔ L. A. MOBBS KETTERING XI

Handed to Nutter-Oldfield Testimonial Fund £ 50 : 17 : 9

Souvenir Card & expression of thanks

To Mr. F. Garley.

for Playing Services.

With the compliments and best wishes from

78, Buccleuch Street
Kettering

Leslie A. Mobbs.

Souvenir card sent to Fred Garley, thanking him for playing in the Albert Nutter and
Norman Oldfield Testimonial held at the North Park.

Ivanhoe: Town League champions 1953
Back Row (l to r): B. Short, A. Small, G. Duck, N. Wardle, J. Chaplin, J. Bent, J.
Hawthorne, R. Drew, M. Beasley, D. Hilliard, D. Hope
Front Row: J. Smith, A. Greensmith, F. Smith, J Newman,
B. Payne, R. Holding, Mr. Townsend.

Taverners A and B: pictured after they had met in the final of the
Six-a-Side tournament in 1976.
Back Row (l to r): F. Beasley, J. Beale, A. Garley, M. Smith, M. Ostle, R. Dexter, J. Sellars
Front Row: S. Weston, B. Foster, T. Lewis, L.Weekes, P. Parker

Chapter XIV

Reflections

When the thoughts run back. I remember once
On this very ground.... Do you hear, my friend?

                                                    G. H. Vallins.

Whilst writing this book I have spoken to many people who have played in
the Town League, some over seventy years ago. There is Fred Blount who,
at the age of eighty-nine, has a memory undimmed by the passing years. He
recalled to me some of the players he played with and against such as Len
and Harry Coe, two brothers who graced the Town League for many years.
Fred also remembered Miss Morris's Bible Class and their remarkable feat
of winning the league three years running. Best of all, he remembers when
he was fielding against Men's Own in a Knock Out match. Fred was
fielding at square leg when the batsman, Harold Townsend, hit the ball hard
towards him and set off for what he considered to be an easy. But he
reckoned without Fred, who pounced on the ball and with one wicket to aim
at smashed it out of the ground to run the Men's Own man out by yards.
        Another Octogenarian is Dennis Hefford. He remembers the Town
League with great affection. Dennis was a very fine cricketer and he was
always immaculately turned out. He played for Havelock Works and Fuller.
I spent several hours in Denise's company and I could have spent many
more just listening to him talking about the league and some of the players of
his generation (some of whom are mentioned in Chapter X11).
        Another man well into his eighties that I spoke to was Reg Green.It
gave me added pleasure to reminisce with Reg because, in 1950, I had the
good fortune to play along side him for Freeman Hardy and Willis when I
was just fifteen years of age. Reg was always a hero of mine and it was great
fun reliving the old days. Reg considered himself to be privileged to play
with the great Maurice Dunkley and he confirmed what a wonderful batsman
he was and that, despite being picked to play for the County, he still
remained a very modest man. Shortly after my visit to Reg, I was extremely
sad to hear that he had passed away. My abiding memory of Reg will be his
infectious love for the game of cricket, and the immense pleasure that he
derived from playing Town League Cricket.
        The three men mentioned above, all began their Town League days
in the 1930s. They were all good cricketers, they were all respected by their
own teams but above all else they were respected by their opponents too.
The one thing that they all had in common was that they all held the Town
League in such high regard. When they spoke about the Town League they

spoke about it with such pleasure and they all echoed the same sentiments..."Those Were the Days".

Writing this book has given me great pleasure but it has also been tinged with a little sadness. During the research for the book I came across many names of people who were dear friends of mine and sadly are no longer with us. Fred Garley was one of these. I never really saw Fred play, but I am assured by the people who did, that he was one of the finest batsmen ever to grace the Town League. Fred would have been embarrassed to read this about himself for he was a modest man, and he was a man of great dignity. He would never stoop to anything underhand and his conduct on and off the field was always impeccable. After he retired from cricket, Fred still gained an enormous amount of pleasure from watching Town League cricket and he was delighted that both his sons, Alan and Brian, also played in the Town League. Fred was also a very good footballer and he played for the Poppies for a number of years.

I first met Bert Garrett when I had finished my national service and I started to play Town League cricket, and we soon forged a friendship which was due, in no small part, to the fact that we both used the Working Men's Club in Wellington Street. Bert became secretary of the Works cricket team and worked tirelessly for the club. He played for Dolcis for many years both before and after the Second World War and he was considered to be a good solid Town League cricketer. Bert spoke to me about many of the players of his time such as the fast bowling attack of Shipley and Meadows who in his words "would put the fear of God into you". Also, Albert Cartwright who, in Bert's opinion, was the finest batsmen he ever saw in the League.

If there was one player who could honestly be described as charismatic it was Alan Coles. Whether he was playing for Old Centralians, Ivanhoe, Working Mens Club, Desborough or Rothwell he had a presence on the field which somehow seemed to undermine the opposition. Alan was a left-handed batsman and he was the hardest hitter of a cricket ball that I ever saw. All bowlers came alike to him and, if it was his day, he could take any attack apart, but he was not a slogger. He would play the ball on its merit, well most of the time anyway. He could play shots all around the wicket and like most good left handers he had the most delightful cover drive. Alan bowled right-handed and in his younger days with the Old Cents and Ivanhoe he would bowl very fast; he would have a run up of something like thirty yards. However, common sense soon prevailed and he cut his run down and proved to be quite an effective bowler. Later in his career he changed to bowling slow leg breaks and he became quite accomplished in the art.

Alan Roberts stood some six feet five tall and he was a bowler who earned the respect of all batsmen in the league. He was fast and he had the ability to get the ball to lift off a length leaving the batsmen to fend it off with, more often than not, disastrous results. He was another righted handed bowler who batted left handed and he was certainly no mug with the bat - sometimes he would open the batting for Ivanhoe. Alan played Town League cricket for over thirty years and he, more than anyone else, typified what the Town League was all about to the working man He would spend five days a week standing at a machine in a shoe factory waiting for Saturday to come around so that he could get out there and play cricket. Then, after the game, he would go for a pint or two or three or four. When he retired from playing cricket he joined Kettering Golf Club and became as popular at golf as he had been at cricket. He was also a well-known local footballer who played for North Park. Big Al, as he was universally known, was one of the most popular men that I ever knew, he did not have an enemy in the world and everyone who knew him only ever spoke of him with kindness and affection, he was truly a "Gentle Giant"

Ron Dolby was a cricket fanatic, so much so, that (in his role as a salesman for Lyons or Crawfords biscuits) if he was working in the Northamptonshire area and the County were playing at home, he would try to get all his calls finished so that he could get to the County ground in Wantage Road in time to see the final session of the days play. Ron was one of those cricketers that you could always rely upon to be on time and to always be well turned out. Although he was not an outstanding cricketer, his enthusiasm for the game rubbed off on you. I shall never forget the time that he turned out for the Works in a league game against Crusaders, a game the Works needed to win to clinch the league title. I cannot remember the actual scores but the upshot was that the Crusaders needed four to win with one wicket to fall. Graham Toseland was taking strike and he was renowned as a big hitter, so needless to say the fielders were dispersed to the boundary, Ron being one of them. Well, Graham got one right in the middle of the bat and sent the ball soaring into the air towards the mid – wicket boundary, it looked for all the world to be going for a certain six. The only fielder going after the ball was Ron and he must have covered a full thirty yards and in sheer desperation, he stuck out his right hand and he caught the ball inches from the line to bring off a most remarkable catch; a catch that won the league for the Works. That catch was to crop up many times over the years and I know Ron was very proud of having played such a vital part in the match - he never tired of people talking about it.

Generally speaking, my memories of the Town League are happy ones and I can still remember that lovely smell you used to get in April when you came across a lawn that had had its first cut of the season and I used to think to myself " It won't be long now." The season would begin with everyone attending net practice on two evenings a week. I well remember the aches and pains we got from using muscles that had been inactive during the winter months. You would wake up the following morning and crawl out of bed and if you dared to cough you would be doubled up with the most excruciating pain.

The Works used the nets at Weekly Glebe for their practice. Some people were gluttons for punishment and one of these was Martin Turner. He was our fast bowler and he thought nothing of having a net and then jogging around the playing field about five times. He once asked me to accompany him and, after about half a lap, I had to feign injury and drop out. On subsequent practice sessions I made sure that I kept as far a way from Martin as I possibly could.

Once the season had started I, and a lot of other cricketers in the Town League, would spend most of the week waiting for Saturdays to come around so that we could get out of the factory and into the fresh air and play cricket. The down side was that if I failed with the bat I was in for a very miserable weekend. It did not matter to me if I managed to take a couple of wickets or to hold on to a good catch, batting was the only important thing and if I should get out for a duck, well that was the end of the world. However, by Tuesday, I had forgotten the previous week's failures and I was already looking forward to the next Saturday.

The Works used to play friendly matches on Sundays and it was not unusual for us to take about forty supporters on the bus with us. Most of our Sunday matches were played away. I remember on one particular Sunday we were playing at Duddington, against Duddington and Tixover and we had an extremely strong batting side that included the likes of Lloyd Weekes, Barry Foster, Barry Essam, Alan Coles and John Lawman; who were all capable of making big scores. We elected to bat first and after about an hour's play we were reduced to a score of 26-8. The next man in at number ten for us was Ivor Wollacott. I should mention, for those of you who did not know Ivor, he was a lovely man, he was full of fun and he always had a smile on his face and he lived life to the full. Well Ivor kept wicket for us and that is why he was in the side - I do not think that he had ever posted a score for us that ran into double figures. Ivor changed all that on this Sunday. He set about the bowling with gusto and all the bowlers came alike to him, he smote them to all parts of the field; some with authentic cricket shots and some that you would not find in any coaching manual. It was a truly remarkable innings and when he reached his fifty everyone was on their feet cheering and clapping, not only in an appreciation of a fine innings but because he was such a popular character and everyone was really pleased for him. That evening the bus stopped at a pub in Weldon, and what a night it was! Ivor, who was an accomplished pianist, entertained the packed pub till closing time. I can still see him sitting at the piano now, with his handkerchief tied around his head with a broad grin of contentment on his face.

I loved the Six-a-Side. The night before the competition I could never get to sleep because I was so worried about over sleeping and not being able to wake in time to play in the first match. Tony Wright, who played for the Centralians, told me that even if he had not been picked to play he would still take his kit down to the North Park in the hope that he could find a team who were a player short, and play for them. This gives you some idea of how keen the players were. When I was the League's secretary I always made a point of getting to the North Park at 9 o'clock on Six-a-Side day. I well remember on one occasion, seeing Stan Leadbetter of Kettering CC helping Cyril Beard to mark out the four wickets that were to be used in the tournament. Just another example of what it meant to the players and how prepared they were to do their bit.

Before I leave the Six-a-Side, I should like to relate to you the day when we were drawn to play our first match at the Weekly Glebe playing Field at 10-30 in the morning, against a team we were expected to beat. Well, so keen was the captain to do well, that he insisted that we got up there by 9 o'clock for some practice. We duly arrived at the appointed hour and had a very good work out that lasted for about an hour. Unfortunately, the best laid plans of mice and men.., and in the ensuing match we were well and truly trounced. Needless to say practising before a match was never mentioned again.

Many people referred to the Town League as the factory or the works league, and certainly from the mid 1930s through to the late 1960s, when there was an abundance of factories in the town, it was quite understandable that it should be thought of as such. When the league first started there were very few factories in the Town - who then made up the teams in the league? In the early days of the league it was the church that provided a goodly number of teams. Amongst these teams were St Mary's BC, St Andrews BC, Miss Butchers BC, Oakley Street BC, Fuller BC, Church Institute, Congregational Church and Men's Own Institute who all provided good support. Kettering has always been well known for its Public houses and its Working Men's Clubs and one would expect these two organizations to provide teams to play in the League and this they surely did. Some of the pubs who entered teams in the League were: Spring Gardens, Robin Hood, Melton Arms, Red Lion (Broughton) and from the clubs we had Athletic Club (Crusaders) Argyle Club, Working Men's Club, Rifle Band Club, North Park Club and Trades Club. These then are the three main areas that accounted for the majority of Town League sides. I have not mentioned the factory sides, as there are far too many to list. However, it is probably worth recounting those teams who for many years were the backbone of the league; Thomas Bird (Dolcis), Freeman Hardy and Willis, Wilson and Watson, Havelock Works (Holyoake), Tite and Garfirth, (Tudors), Perfecta, Timpsons and KICS (Kaycee, Glebe). There are other teams who did not fit into the above categories such as Old Centralians, (who were the league's most successful team), Electricity Board, Gas Board, British Railway and Barton Seagrave, to name just a few. So it was not just a factory League, it was a League that embraced people from different backgrounds and from all walks of life.

Many people ask the same question, why did the Town League fold? The simple answer would seem to be, that it folded because there were not enough people interested to keep the League going. I think, however that you have to dig a little deeper than this to find the cause. When the league was at its strongest in the 1940s, 50s and 60s, the majority of the people of the town did not own motor cars. They were therefore restricted to leisure activities closer to home. I am sure that this was the main consideration taken into account when the Town League was formed and it proved to be an ideal solution to solving the lack of mobility. Transport was not the only reason. As I have mentioned earlier in this chapter, there were many factories, clubs and pubs in the town and gradually they formed teams and, as the number of teams increased, the rivalry between the various organizations also increased. It was a healthy rivalry, it was intense but, at the end of the day, it was always played in a friendly manner and in the true spirit of the game. Today, nearly all the factories in the town have closed down, most of the clubs have gone, the old fashioned public houses that we used to frequent, with the exception of a few, no longer exist. I think this is the biggest single factor that is responsible for the demise of the Town League. Another factor that obviously had an effect on the League is that we live in a much more affluent society today and today's youngsters are spoilt for choice. Sadly the situation is not helped by the fact that most schools do not have cricket as part of the school curriculum, and it is sad to think that, what was once regarded as our national game, has been virtually discarded by our schools.

"If I had my time to live over again" is the opening line to an old song. Well, if I had my time over again there are many changes that I would make. However, the one thing that I definitely would not want to change is my time in the Town League. I derived a great deal of enjoyment and pleasure from the League, and where else would I have been able to make so many friends, not just amongst my own team mates, but with the opposition as well. I can still remember the great matches and the not so great ones, the celebrations when we won and drowning our sorrows when we lost. After

the match had finished we would walk to the nearest drinking house and partake of a little liquid refreshment. At closing time we went to the nearest chippie or Chinese, (that is if any of us had any money left), then we would wind our weary way home with a (quickly going cold) peace offering.
"If I had my time to live over again....."

FIRST DIVISION CHAMPIONS

1912	Men's Own & W Men's Club		1952	Fuller Institute
1913	Kettering Midland Railway		1953	Ivanhoe
1913	Miss Butcher's Bible Class		1954	Old Centralians
1914	Working Men's Club		1955	Athletic
1915	No Competition		1956	Ivanhoe
1916	No Competition		1957	Old Centralians
1917	No Competition		1958	Old Centralians
1919	No Competition		1959	Old Centralians I
1920	Men's Own Institute		1960	Old Centralians I
1921	Athletic Club		1961	Ivanhoe
1922	Men's Own Institute		1962	Working M C
1923	No Competition		1963	Old Centralians I
1924	Men's Own Institute		1964	Working M C I
1925	North Park		1965	Old Centralians I
1926	S. Patricks		1966	Working M C I
1927	S. Patricks		1967	British Legion
1928	St Marys Bible Class		1968	British Legion
*1929	F. H and Willis		1969	British Legion
	Miss Butchers		1970	Crusaders
*1930	F. H and Willis		1971	Taverners
	St. Mary's BC		1972	Taverners
1931	Working Mens Club II		1973	Casuals
1932	Thomas Birds		1974	Old Centralians I
1933	Wilson & Watson		1975	Crusaders
1934	Havelock Works		1976	Crusaders
1935	Thomas Birds		1977	Crusaders
1936	Miss Butchers B C		1978	Tudors
1937	Miss Butchers B C		1979	Jumbos
1938	Miss Butchers B C		1980	Christie Colts
1939	Thomas Bird		1981	Tudors
1940	St Mary's Bible Class		1982	Tudors
1941	No Competition		1983	Tudors
1942	No Competition		1984	Jumbos
1943	No Competition		1985	Mercenaries
1944	No Competition		1986	Wellingb. Indians
1945	No Competition		1987	Wellingb. Indians
1946	Rifle Band Club		1988	Holyoake
1947	Dolcis		1989	Saracens
1948	F H & W		1990	Bletsoe
1949	British Electricity		1991	Crusaders
1950	Fuller Institute		1992	Bletsoe
1951	British Electricity		1993	Crusaders

* Denotes A year when the first division consisted of Division IA and Division IB.

SECOND DIVISION CHAMPIONS

1921	Barton Wanderers	1961	Working Men's Club
1938	Barton Wanderers	1962	Nomads
1939	Gravestocks	1963	Casuals
1940	Freeman Hardy & Willis	1964	William Timpsons
1949	Wilson & Watsons	1965	Venturers
1950	Old Centralians	1966	Dolcis
*1951	(Div II A) Kaycee	1967	Tite & Garirth
*1951	(Div II B) F. H and Willis	1968	William Timpsons
*1952	(Div II A) Athletic	1969	Dolcis
*1952	(Div II B) British Railways	1970	Casuals
*1953	(Div II A) British Legion	1971	Holyoake
*1953	(Div II B) Staples Printers	1972	Tite and Garfirth
1954	Havelock Works	1973	Wellingb. Indians
1955	Holyoake	1974	Taverners II
1956	William Timpsons	1982	Old Centralians
1957	Foresters	1983	Kangos
1958	Kaycee	1984	Merceneries
1959	Old Centralians II		
1960	Working Men's Club		

You will notice that there are years when there were insufficient teams to run more than one league, hence the gaps.

* Denotes A year when the Second Division consisted of Div IIA and Div IIB

THIRD DIVISION CHAMPIONS

1955	Dolcis	1962	Tite and Garfirth
1956	Spring Gardens	1963	Keystone
1961	Nomads	1964	Dolcis

ABBOTT CUP WINNERS

1967	Crusaders & B. Legion	1981	Tudors
1968	Casuals	1982	Jumbos
1969	Taverners	1983	Tudors
1970	Old Centralians	1984	Flamingos
1971	Taveners	1985	Wellingb. Indians
1972	Taverners	1986	Crusaders
1973	Wellingborough Indians	1987	Flamingos
1974	Old Centralians 1	1988	Tudors
1975	Crusaders	1989	Bletsoe
1976	Simbas	1990	Bletsoe
1977	Crusaders	1991	Tudors
1978	Crusaders & Jumbos	1992	Bletsoe
1979	Tudors	1993	Crusaders
1980	Jumbos		

KETTERING ASSOCIATION KNOCKOUT CUP WINNERS

1929	Mens Own Institute	1958	Southgate
1930	Mens Own Institute	1959	Kettering
1931	North Park	1960	Southgate
1932	Frank Wrights	1961	Kettering
1933	Frank Wrights	1962	Kettering
1934	Frank Wrights	1963	Kettering
1935	William Timpsons	1964	Wanderers
1936	Kettering	1965	Kettering
1937	Freeman Hardy & Willis	1966	Old Centralians
1938	Mobbs & Lewis	1967	Working Men's Club
1939	Freeman Hardy & Willis	1968	Kettering
1940	William Timpsons	1969	Kettering
1941	Men's Own Institute	1970	Kettering
1942	Men's Own Institute	1971	Kettering
1943	Men's Own Institute	1972	Taverners
1944	Royal Air Force	1973	Taverners
1945	Geddington	1974	Kettering
1946	Nomads	1975	Taverners
1947	Men's Own Institute	1976	Great Oakley
1948	Old Cytringanians	1977	Kettering
1949	Kettering	1978	Kettering
1950	Old Cytringanians	1979	Kettering
1951	W. B. Wrights	1980	Kettering
1952	British Railways	1981	Kettering
1953	Kettering	1982	Isham
1954	Barton Seagrave	1983	Weekly & Warkton
1955	Kettering	1984	No Competition
1956	Athletic	1985	Great Oakley
1957	Kettering		

THE EDGAR TOWELL CHALLENGE CUP

1955	Athletic	1975	Brixworth
1956	Old Cytringanians	1976	Taverners
1957	Kettering	1977	Taverners
1958	Crusaders	1978	Casuals
1959	William Timpsons	1979	Barton Seagrave A
1960	Old Centralians A	1980	Weekley & Warkton
1961	Ivanhoe	1981	Brixworth
1962	Kettering	1982	Brixworth
1963	Kettering	1983	Juventus
1964	Crusaders	1984	Weekley & Warkton
1965	Old Centralians A	1985	Taverners Old Boys
1966	Keystone	1986	Holyoake
1967	Kettering B	1987	Overstone
1968	Barton Seagrave	1988	Overstone
1969	Taverners	1989	Mikado
1970	British Legion	1990	Wellingborough I.C.S.
1971	Taverners	1991	Wellingb. Indians
1972	Christie Colts	1992	Mikado
1973	Taverners	1993	Wellingb. Indians
1974	Kettering	1994	Harrowden

CENTURIES IN THE TOWN LEAGUE

Score	Player	Date	Team	Opponents
150	Mark Hanby	1993	Venturers	Foresters
150	Mark Wittering	1993	Tudors	Venturers
144 *	Mark Mason	1990	Ram Sports	Saracens
133	Dave Fenwick	1990	Crusaders	Saracens
125	Dave Fenwick	1990	Crusaders	Mill Road
121	Mick Beasley	1964	Holyoake	Old Centralians I
121	Lloyd Weekes	1967	Holyoake	Old Centralians I
121	Steve Bailey	1987	Harlequin	Brentmere
120	Steve Bailey	1987	Harlequin	Venturers
117*	Reg Green	1947	F.H.& Willis	Havelock Works
114	G. Wallington	1938	Gravestocks	Wilson & Watsons
112*	Dean Pridmore	1991	Venturers	Mill Road II
107	John Warwick	1991	Tudors	Mill Road II
106	D. Spriggs	1959	M. & Feltons	Dolcis
105*	John Kemp	1990	Ram Sports	Saracens
105	Reg Green	1939	F.H. & Willis	M.& Lewis
105	Ray Pell	1951	Havelock Works	M.& Lewis
104*	Arthur Sellars	1950	Old Cents I	Perfecta
104*	Roy Briggs	1957	Old Cents II	Perfecta
104	Mark Wittering	1990	Tudors	Saracens
104	Tony Wright	1967	Old Cents	Dolcis
104*	A. Cartwright	1936	Thomas Birds	Kaycee
103*	Joe Bent	1950	Fuller	British Legion
103*	P. Jami	1983	Kangos	Christie Colts
103	K. Patel	1989	Kangos	Holyoake
103	Bert Russell	1933	Havelock Works	Thomas Birds
103	Steve Bailey	1991	Bletsoe	Saracens
102	M. Dunkley	1933	F. H.Willis	Miss Butchers
102	Steve Kendall	1988	Ram Sports	Venturers
102	Peter Daniel	1990	Tudors	Saracens
102	Neil Mobbs	1986	Melton	Harlequin
101	W. Julian	1938	Gravestocks	Gas Company
101*	Joe Bent	1971	T. & Garfirth	Taverners II
101*	L. Hales	1933	Wilson & W.	Havelock Works
100	Albert Smith	1963	Keystone BC	Perfecta
100*	Charlie Richards	1953	Casuals	British Railway
100	David Beale	1986	Holyoake	Flamingos
100	Ken Gully	1987	Crusaders	Venturers
100	Roger Fox	1990	Bletsoe	
100	Gordon Livesy	1962	Keystone BC	Venturers

*not out

OUT IN THE NERVOUS NINETIES

Score	Player	Date	Team	Opponents
99	H. Simcoe	1952	GPO	Perfecta
98	B. Bambridge	1982	Venturers	Christie Colts
96	J. Hilliard	1966	Holyoake	Barton B
96	D. Fenwick	1992	Crusaders	East Carlton
94	S. Patel	1987	Kangos	Crusaders
93	M. Beale	1985	Holyoake	Crusaders
92	F. Garley	1949	G.T. Whites	Wilson & W
92	F. Sismey	1952	British Legion	Perfecta
91	J. Kemp	1990	Ram Sports	Saracens
90	R. Pringle	1966	Nomads	Venturers
90	S. Walton	1978	Christie Colts	Venturers
90	K. Ashik	1985	WICC II	Mercaneries

BEST BOWLING PERFORMANCES

Player	Team	Opponents	Wickets	Year
O. Pearson	North Park	Thom Birds	10-12	1930
S. Dholakia	Old Cents II	Christie Colts	10-14	1973
T. Holmes	Dolcis	Taverners	10-24	1968
P. Payne	Fuller	Casuals	10-26	1951
W. Dunham	Mobbs & Lewis	Wilson & W	10-48	1935
R. Walpole	Crusaders	Christie Colts	10-49	1983
D. Newman	Crusaders	Kangos	10-50	1981
Gilbert Duck	Ivanhoe	Railway	9-2	1955
P. Rowney	G.P.O.	Keystone	9-13	1968
K. Brock	Red Lion	Venturers	9-17	1988
J. Gamble	Ivanhoe	Old Cents	9-20	1961
I. Mason	Holyoake	Brentmere	9-20	1982
A. Roberts	W.M.C	Old Cents	9-25	1963
K. Patel	Kangos	Saracens	9-26	1990
T. Flak	Crusaders	Holyoake	9-27	1983
T. Hyam	Staples	Old Cents II	9-28	1951
C. Howard	Kaycee	Old Cents II	9-38	1956
G. Short	W.M.C.	Old Cents II	9-41	1961
J. Lawman	British Legion	Crusaders	8-4	1969
G. Short	WMC II	Dolcis	8-4	1965
S. Stokes	Saracens	Mill Road	8-4	1991
J. Bent	Fuller	British Railway	8-4	1950
J. Newman	Fuller	Miss Butchers	8-8	1939
D. Bellamy	Venturers	Christie Colts	8-8	1982
W. Beasley	Nomads	Kaycee	8-12	1953
H. Liquorish	Mens Own	Trades Club	8-12	1924
P. Mann	Old Centralians I	British Legion	8-13	1958
T. Freeman	Men's Own	Miss Butchers	8-14	1924
W, Woolmer	Freeman Hardy	Miss Butchers	8-16	1929
F. Smith	Ivanhoe	Freeman Hardy	8-16	1953
L. Cullip	Thomas Birds	Miss Butchers	8-17	1938
J. Law	M & Lewis	Kaycee	8-18	1936
C. Ingram	Dolcis	Electricians	8-20	1950
F. Lawrence	Casuals	Venturers	8-20	1969
B. Bambridge	Venturers	Brentmere	8-20	1981
K. Allbright	Casuals	Keystone	8-22	1968
F. Lawrence	Casuals	Four Seasons	8-22	1970
K. Allbright	Casuals	Old Cents II	8-22	1975
T. Holmes	Crusaders	Jumbos	8-22	1977
D. Simmons	Barton B	Argyll	8-23	1972
C. Sherbourne	Freeman Hardy	Miss Butchers	8-25	1934

Player	Team	Opponents	Wickets	Year
L. Shipley	Thomas Birds	Kaycee	8-26	1935
P. Rowney	GPO	Munn & Feltons	8-26	1955
S. Bailey	Bletsoe	East Carlton	8-27	1992
W. Dunham	M & Lewis	Freeman Hardy	8-28	1939
R. Smith	Tudors	Simba II	8-28	1975
K. Brock	Mill Road II	Mill Road I	8-28	1991
R. Pell	Havelock W	Athletic	8-32	1951
B. Garrett	Dolcis	Tite & Garfirth	8-33	1952
L. Smith	Saracens	Kangos	8-36	1991
I Addis	M & Lewis	British Legion	8-53	1953
R. Pell	Havelock W	Ivanhoe	8-54	1956

PLAYERS WHO HAVE ACHIEVED HAT TRICKS

Player	Team	Opponents	Year
H. K. Wilson	British Legion	W.M.C. II	1922
O. Pearson	North Park	Thomas BirdS	1930
E. Groome	Nomads	Mobbs & Lewis	1949
D. Chaplin	Mens Own	Fuller	1950
G. Duck	Fuller	Dolcis	1952
F. Lawrence	Casuals	Mobbs & Lewis	1956
M.Tyrrell	Tite & Garfirth	Old Centralians II	1959
P. Mann	Old Centralians	Glebe	1960
E. Dawkins	Dolcis	Barton B	1969
J. Bent	Tite & Garfirth	Taverners II	1971
M. Ward	Nomads	Taverners	1973
T. Holmes	Crusaders	Jumbos	1977
J. Hill	Holyoake	Old Centralians II	1978
Manhar Patel	Flamingos	Tudors	1983
M. Chapman	Tudors	Old Centralians II	1984
R. Smith	Tudors	Brentmere	1986
P. Gamble	Tudors	Melton	1986
D. Strangeward	Bletsoe	Venturers	1989
K. Patel	Kangos	Bletsoe	1989
P Eaton	Ram Sports	Saracens	1990
D. Holmes	Crusaders	Mill Road	1991
M. Langley	Ram Sports	Crusaders	1992